HOW THE BICYCLE SHONE

Gillian Allnutt was born in 1949 in London but spent half of her childhood in Newcastle upon Tyne. In 1988 she returned to live in the North East. Before that, she read Philosophy and English at Cambridge and then spent the next 17 years living mostly in London, working mostly as a part-time teacher in further and adult education but also as a performer, publisher, journalist and freelance editor. From 1983 to 1988 she was Poetry Editor at *City Limits* magazine.

Her collections *Nantucket and the Angel* and *Lintel* were both shortlisted for the T.S. Eliot Prize. Poems from these collections are included in her Bloodaxe retrospective *How the Bicycle Shone: New & Selected Poems* (2007), which draws on six published books plus a new collection, *Wolf Light*, and was a Poetry Book Society Special Commendation. Her most recent collections, both from Bloodaxe, are *indwelling* (2013) and *wake* (2018). She has also published *Berthing: A Poetry Workbook* (NEC/Virago, 1991), and was co-editor of *The New British Poetry* (Paladin, 1988).

From 2001 to 2003 she held a Royal Literary Fund Fellowship at Newcastle and Leeds Universities. She won the Northern Rock Foundation Writer's Award in 2005 and received a Cholmondeley Award in 2010. Since 1983 she has taught creative writing in a variety of contexts, mainly in adult education and as a writer in schools. In 2009/10 she held a writing residency with The Medical Foundation for the Care of Victims of Torture (now Freedom From Torture) in the North East, working with asylum seekers in Newcastle and Stockton. In 2013/14 she taught creative writing to undergraduates on the Poetry and Poetics course in the English Department of Durham University. She lives in Co. Durham.

Gillian Allnutt was awarded the Queen's Gold Medal for Poetry 2016. The Medal is given for excellence in poetry and was presented to her by The Queen.

GILLIAN ALLNUTT

How the Bicycle Shone

NEW & SELECTED POEMS

BLOODAXE BOOKS

Copyright © Gillian Allnutt
1981, 1987, 1994, 1997, 2001, 2004, 2007

ISBN: 978 1 85224 759 1

First published 2007 by
Bloodaxe Books Ltd,
Eastburn,
South Park,
Hexham,
Northumberland NE46 1BS.

www.bloodaxebooks.com
For further information about Bloodaxe titles
please visit our website or write to
the above address for a catalogue.

Supported using public funding by
ARTS COUNCIL
ENGLAND

Cover design: Neil Astley & Pamela Robertson-Pearce.

Digital reprint of the 2007 Bloodaxe Books edition.

For Christine Holloway

ACKNOWLEDGEMENTS

This book includes poems selected from Gillian Allnutt's collections *Spitting the Pips Out* (Sheba, 1981), *Beginning the Avocado* (Virago, 1987), *Blackthorn* (Bloodaxe Books, 1994) and *Nantucket and the Angel* (Bloodaxe Books, 1997), as well as the whole of *Lintel* (Bloodaxe Books, 2001), *Sojourner* (Bloodaxe Books, 2004) and a collection of new poems, *Wolf Light* (2007).

Acknowledgements are due to the editors of the following publications in which some of the poems from *Wolflight* first appeared: *Images of Women* (Arrowhead Press, 2006), *Poetraits* (Graham Kershaw, 2003), *Poetry*, *The Rialto* and *Southlight*. Some poems have also appeared online at www.acknowledgedland.com and at www.blinking-eye.co.uk.

Some of the poems were first published in *Hob Green* (Phoenix Poetry Pamphlets, Grand Phoenix Press, 2004).

Thanks, as ever, to Writing from the Inside Out, the women's writing workshop based in Newcastle upon Tyne, where many of my poems begin.

Huge thanks to the Northern Rock Foundation for the Northern Rock Foundation Writer's Award 2005, allowing me to write for three years without distractions.

CONTENTS

FROM **NANTUCKET AND THE ANGEL** (1997)

LINTEL (2001)

SOJOURNER (2004)

from

SPITTING THE PIPS OUT

(1981)

Words to her Lover

I shall keep this bit for God, she said,
tucking it away.

It could be a flower
or a star, a wooden spoon, rice
paper, the shine of the river
a common or garden stone –

You cannot see inside a stone, she said.

It could be a moth
or a stamp with an African bird on it
a word I have forgotten
or a thin cloth folded like a handkerchief
a leaf just looking
or the trick of an eyelid dreaming
a drop of cream, an apple
and a book on a rainy day
a wooden doll with one leg broken since my birthday
or a thread in the eye of a needle.

Desist, she said,
mocking his open fist.

I have given you my bones to keep.
I will sleep like the earth in you.
I've given you my eyes, though they are stones,
my apple heart with its green sleeves.
I'll sing you a song like a river flowing,
give you the sea that grieves in me
like broken things forgotten.
I would stir the earth for you
like a great wind blowing.

But I am going where the moon goes now
when she has finished sewing up the sky
and sits and eats stars
on the other side.

Give me the wooden spoon
so I can eat my curds and whey, she said,
tucking in.

a poem for my mother

the sky is the quiet blue
colour of mary's faded cotton frock

carpenter's wife picking the splinters
out of her husband's fingers

and I am thinking quietly
about you

      who played Chopin
less perfectly than Rubinstein

I remember your difficult bits
as if somewhere the grass got into a knot

or the moon cricked her neck very slightly
and everything was all right

clockmender's wife picking the cogs and wheels
out of the boiling pan

before the sky walks quietly
into another ordinary dawn

'mother you never told me how to mend'

mother you never told me how to mend
the invisible hole   the soul
worn thin with wondering

all the world's a sheet
and all the women in it   here to turn
sides to middle   when it gets torn   to begin
all over again with a snitch of thread

mother I cannot lie down in this bed   riddled with stitches
the pinned bones of the spine itch

it does not do and it does not do
to sit all day and sew

the light of another world filters through
these bare threads

the eye of the needle opens wide
to admit me

for a friend gardening

today you are
digging over your thoughts
like an autumn garden   imagining
next spring   as a lawn
for stretching out
a new person

from

BEGINNING THE AVOCADO

(1987)

Ode

To depict a (bicycle), you must first come to love (it).
ALEKSANDR BLOK

I swear by every rule in the bicycle
owner's manual

that I love you, I, who have repeatedly,
painstakingly,

with accompanying declaration of despair,
tried to repair

you, to patch things up,
to maintain a workable relationship.

I have spent sleepless nights
in pondering your parts – those private

and those that all who walk the street
may look at –

wondering what makes you tick
over smoothly, or squeak.

O my trusty steed,
my rusty three-speed,

I would feed you the best oats
if oats

were applicable.
Only linseed oil

will do
to nourish you.

I want
so much to paint

you,
midnight blue

mudgutter black
and standing as you do, ironic

at the rail
provided by the Council –

beautiful
the sun caught in your back wheel –

or at home in the hall, remarkable
among other bicycles,

your handlebars erect.
Allow me to depict

you thus. And though I can't do justice
to your true opinion of the surface

of the road –
put into words

the nice distinctions that you make
among the different sorts of tarmac –

still I'd like to set the record of our travels straight.
I'd have you know that

not with three-in-one
but with my own

heart's
spittle I anoint your moving parts.

convent

a fistful of notes
my heart

a thin must
covers the keyboard of ivory soldiers

girls are expected
to wear gloves

and a labour of love is lost
in plain sewing

each finger stitched
to the palm

the loose hem of the street
catches me

the tune
of a barrel organ

the monkey
playing alone

streetheart
no penny can buy it

I ought
to give my pocket

money for a poor child
going begging in the east

in the name of the father the son
and the monkey goes on

like the ghost
of a tell tale tit your heart shall be split

while the bell rings for angelus
here are gloves of silk   a purse

on a string
worn over the shoulder

and nothing
in it

after prayers
there will be bread and butter soldiers

a measure of milk
plainsong

Two Sketches
(for Monica and Alice)

1 *Hiroshima, 1945*

Kasa promises. She walks
carefully all the way back
from the shop.

She has one foot on the step
when the sun slips. Her shadow stops.
She looks up.

The sun
does not fall down
until late in the afternoon.

That is a promise. It has been
given to us.
It is only eight fifteen.

She is bringing a bottle of rice wine.
It is precious.
There will be a celebration.

The house is gone.
Kasa stops. There is a shadow on the step
looking up.

Alice examines the shadow
that lies before her
like a future.

It is fantastic:
an elegant woman dressed in black,
an old one bent over a stick.

Alice stops short.
She is only eight,
but she can just imagine it.

Alice, come on up.
The sun has reached the bottom of the step.
It is quarter past eight.

Tomorrow is
another day. That is a promise.
Come.

Alice forgets her shadow. Carelessly
it hops before her
two steps at a time.

At Dinner

Sophia, I have not forgiven anyone.
I called them my friends who, over dinner, called
for talk of the trouble in South Africa.

Airy and thin as bone china
was their conversation, their political acumen quick
as knives and forks of stainless steel.

Women of damask, Cambridge men, there is blood on my hands.
They were kind to you, my friend.
They asked no questions.

Sophia, what were you pondering in your heart?
You smiled that night, I remember,
and folded your napkin with care.

after a year the cherry blossom is here again
(for John)

I remember ironing my dress

the formal statement
                        Bach sonata drawn
from one violin in the quiet meetinghouse
brightness caught in a high window

they laid you under the grass   I remember
the formal emotion   our bone stiff standing   thinking
are we old enough to know this
where is sadness

I for hours holding a battered cigarette
in a cold hand   match after match going out
in a scattering wind
                        the cherry flowers mad with it

Alien

> *... as a woman I have no country.*
> VIRGINIA WOOLF

I have never returned
wounded, to the white cliffs
of Dover, knowing I rule –
though a bit of shrapnel
is my heart –
over and over singing
Elizabeth and England
in the bottom of
a gunboat.

No. I walk these streets
already beautifully paved
with bones of enemies
and women. I am subject
to a proud succession,
brave and noble sons
in mufti, bowler hats.

Who point to our great poets
with their walking sticks
of oak. Who will not bury
my heart in Westminster Abbey,
singing God the Father God
the Son and God the Holy Ghost,
this morning the serving maid
burned the toast.

Eliza sits below stairs to mend
the linen here in England's
green and pleasant –

and this land is my land
to which I have never returned.

Epiphany (Yorkshire Dales)
(for John)

Solitude   your death   a drover's
road   two dry stone walls   the borders
of the earth   each stone a hand's width and the berth of God

Where blackthorn lays the wind bare to the bone
you herded stars

Why Not
(for Virginia Woolf, Sylvia Plath, Marina Tsvetayeva)

Still, I wait.
I cannot say it is love stops short
of the rope
or the river
the quiet caress of gas in an uncaring winter.
What then?

For I have stood by the indifferent river, choosing
the plunge
or the same walk home through the lengthening valley,
unstrengthened, holding a stone sagged
with the damp weight of the year
and fear articulating my heart
words held toneless in the teeth of the air.

And yes, taking charred cakes from the oven
intended for tea – I have tried
to see my head on the slatted shelf,
my old raw self gone in a whiff of gas
through a crack in the kitchen door,
my words in a clattered heap on the cold floor
like broken cups –
not hearing the children want more.

I still hold to the rope
that could silence the last obstinate scratch in the air.
A catch in the throat –
if I knew how,
I could quicken the quiet creak of despair
no more.

It is dark here
but it's only a crack in the pavement.
As yet words find their own way out
and I sit tight, striking matches.
Perhaps I shall go on like a cigarette
watching my ashes grow
and my small tongue of fire slow, tire.

I draw on life and wait
for the abrupt stubbing out.

the house of the dead
(for John)

your death left the door of the world wide open

stars began to come in   like lepers
home again

deadbody peppercorns   already dust
they are the burnt out images of love
you left behind   exhausted

there *is* a way out of this house   you said

but they brought your body to its shrivelled home

and I must call in the cold stars
warm them

Mary at Golgotha

No one can mend this
hill where the wind knows
no boundaries. The skull is
with God, the soul's thread
broken. Here

and there a star recalls
birth, a child falls somewhere
close to the earth, the mild grass
stitches up small holes and tatters
carefully.

With rags and bones a man
repairs the scattered
self, forgets this place
and sleeps.

For me, the moon's face, scarred
with resurrection, knows
there is no simple
sewing up: my own scars opening
and opening like eyes, devour
forgetfulness.

Lizzie Siddall: Her Journal (1862)

(for John)

INTRODUCTION

Elizabeth Eleanor Siddall (1829-62) was the daughter of an ironmonger who later kept a shop in the Old Kent Road in London. At first apprenticed to a milliner, she was then taken up as a model by the young Pre-Raphaelite painters, posing for many of their pictures at the standard rate of a shilling an hour. She was the model for Rossetti's 'Beata Beatrix', and for the drowned 'Ophelia' – for which painting she floated fully-clothed in a bath, becoming ill as a result.

She was not "beautiful" by Victorian standards: she had straight red hair and a plain round face with pointed features, hooded eyes and a long upper lip. Rossetti, and the other painters, "recreated" her as a Pre-Raphaelite Woman: she lamented, 'No one cares about my soul'.

She expressed a desire to draw and thereby aroused Rossetti's interest. Eventually he married her. (On the marriage certificate her father's occupation was put down as 'optician'.) But the marriage was short-lived: Lizzie Siddall was not healthy, became addicted to laudanum and died of an overdose. With his wife, Rossetti buried his poems to her: seven years later he had her exhumed in order to retrieve the poems. It was said that her red hair was still bright.

1

Pre-Raphaelite, they say: I sit for hours
and peer at painted women in a book,
peer as into mirrors
lest my face forsake

me, and the fable of my hair,
and I not fit
the cap I often wear
so ill in his peculiarly silent heart.

2

I said to him today, I'd love to draw –
no, not another angel
but the likeness of my own poor
soul.

I think it like the moon,
a plain round saucer
or the bottom of a shallow pan.
I am the daughter of an ironmonger.

When he married me
he made the man
behind the counter write out carefully
'optician'

and he spelled it slowly for him.
I remember the morning my father died.
They said I made a prim –
a proper bride.

They had already paid me
a shilling an hour
to be
who was it now – Ophelia. Ophelia

died
by her own fair hand
they said. They made
believe she drowned

as I did in that bath
they brought me to day after day: I
held my breath
so long, I thought I would die

too. I was afraid
when they spoke of the beautiful
dead
woman in the book. They thought of her soul,

not mine,
dragged under by my own hair and the dress
I put on
every day. For better, for worse

I dared
this afternoon
to say to him in one of his indifferent moods
that I should like to be alone

awhile –
'as lonely as the moon is' – wistful phrases
please him. I said nothing of my soul,
of course.

3

'Copperknob'
my father always said,
giving the kettle a good hard rub
and 'Go to bed

now, Lizzie, or you'll lose
the lovely red
of your hair. No man will choose
you, though you thread

the finest needle
between here and Mayfair.
Look after it, girl.'
I was rare

enough to him, a sight
for sore eyes used
to the long dim days in the shop, and bright
as a kettle in the dust

behind the counter
where I played.
These days rarer, father – all those pictures –
and I think perhaps I should have stayed

at home where I belonged.
Here is a housemaid and her
row of warming pans. I may not lend
a hand to anyone. I live here with my red hair,

buried
far beneath it. It betrays
me to him. But inside
me, something tries

to live,
as if it were my own child turning
in her grave
and still, my wild red hair will go on keening,

shining
for him. Father, call me
home on kettle cleaning
day.

4

'Come to bed
now, Lizzie, do'
he pleads –
but I am slow

with buttons, slow to braid
my hair.
It is hard
to leave the mirror

alone. I do not know who I am
without her
whose loveliness is everything to him.
I am spare

in soul. I leave
my body
beautiful to him who makes believe
he beds a lady.

Beatrice may be
the one
who can undo her body
like a button,

who can let him
in
to his dream.
Unknowing and unknown,

I am beyond
the pale
and lovely land
of lady. Wakeful

now, I wait
for morning light, the bright mane of her hair
to burn out
of the mirror.

5

In bare grey light he slept
like a saint.
I crept
into his empty room – and that paint

woman was grinning as if she had risen
from the grave –
as if she had removed the stone
of love

that laid her
tenderly in earth,
that stayed her
hand, her mouth –

as if she, grinning, had grown
out of him,
had gripped the bone
of Adam

in her teeth
and stripped it of its dream,
as if at last she'd torn the truth
from him

and laughed at his little
death, alone,
and laid her lovely head upon the pale
grey stone.

She beckoned me to come
plain as I was in my nightdress,
and gave me her own name,
Beatrice.

Late this afternoon I stole
into the room
again – but she, subdued and sorrowful,
looked only out from the little window of his dream.

6

Laudanum
is half
a honeymoon – and by my little window blows laburnum,
morning brief

euphoria, the hour of butter
milk. But then the windblown
waterlight withdraws. The long dour
afternoon

grows over me, a hood, a close brown pod
and I –
my soul, my sun, my seed –
am poisoned inly.

7

She has been his
bedded
Beatrice.
He'll have his dead

soul soon enough.
Dante Gabriel's
wife
is far from well,

a walking shadow. Shorn of his wild
desire,
she fades as do the lilies of the field.
Only her hair is still on fire.

8

I, Lizzie, once a girl
growing up in the Old Kent Road,
give my soul
to God

the ironmonger.
Send word
to my father
when I am dead.

Being True

(for John)

You have returned yourself to bone
my shadow. Self

protective of me, still, to say –

when often, then,
I turned myself away
from you –

I loved you. My embattled shadow
burns.

I shall not spare
myself the loss
of you.

I bless you and the long bare road
begins.

am I

to go alone into the dark
interior   impenetrable home
of root and shard and stone   I am
afraid to come into my own
dour garden of desire   no dream
dispels me   here   it is my own heart
I explore   the loss of that
penultimate   my name

for laura   two weeks old

our children are borrowed
the old woman said
she had never heard of god

as if you had already
dwelt one hundred years
on earth   you are

a bit bewildered
lost in your red wrinkled skin
and just too tired

to listen to us
who have borrowed a name
for you   a hand me down

who are you   apart
from laura

the souls of the dead
inhabit the red bean   said
the egyptians   darkly

and who am I
being here and now blind
to all but laura   to say

that some old soul
did not set out
to be

found
among bulrushes
or in the shadow of the bean tree

apart from laura
who are we

my soul is a dark blue stone

Kirovakan, 1971

my soul is a dark blue stone

armenian

and could have happened to anyone walking
on that hard, particular mountain

only would, for the life of me, imagine

and must still, mistakenly
in my worried hand

North Norfolk

This is great grandmother's garden, the flint
ground of her being.   The roodscreen
faces of her saints are diligent, thin.
Her church windows are plain.
God grows out of doors among the tares and stones.
The best of him must go to the malting.
Frost and a bracing wind begot her faith, a plough
share of truth.   The sky is her gaunt grace, her place beneath it
bounded by rivers of reed and alder
and the flint grey sea.

when the rain
(for Sarah)

when the rain
comes slow   which may be the way
Ruth came through a field of shards   and the world is
no longer a woman gleaning
what little she can from the wind   when the untold
earth sits spinning a cocoon of green
vine like a long yarn
round and round the garden   my old mother
knows   even the stones
are opening

Reply to your card from the Greek Islands
(for Christine)

You mention the poppies: it was this time
of the year we waited together
in Crete, for cars to take us over
the dry stone mountains, waited for water,
watched the remote white-painted houses
for signs. It was so hot sometimes
I was afraid.

I'd forgotten the ruins, had almost forgotten you
reading aloud from the guide, your discoveries
turning a footnote into a stone
half-buried in holy ground.

I remember us there, by the road, and always
the poppies blowing along the side
of the wind.

Beginning the avocado

My heart is an avocado
stone in a pot
of earth

but my old truth
my stubborn Elizabeth, my queen
is gone.

She's taken a bath
without telling. The stone
remembers

to root
me in another time
but when

the poem itself splits
open, letting
in

death, the watering
hole of a queen, how am I
to go on?

from

BLACKTHORN

(1994)

Bringing the Geranium in for the Winter

Almost dark, the rain begins
again. I steal into my own
October garden

with a small black bucketful of
compost and a trowel.
I kneel

as if you, beautiful
before time with your small pale flowers still
opening, were my soul

and God,
in spite of groundfrost
and the book of rules for growing,

could
exist, incomprehensible, companion of
the overcoming darkness in the grass and apple garden.

I return among the small grave stones
I made your borders with
to kneel, to feel

about, to, probing, put my trowel in, pull you from
your unmade bed,
your mad

dishevelled garden: lifted out of,
orphaned bit of
truth

your petals wet with
rain. It's rain I somehow am
no longer stiff with

now my hands
the barest hands I have
are briefly of this earth and have begun

to learn the part of
root and leaf
to live

with
potting and repotting.
So I set

you, lastly, in the dry
companionable kitchen
on a plate,

my table
laid with cloth of quiet
October light.

heart note

because we for a while had been living there my heart

thought it was a house with cupboards and an open fire
and a door giving onto
an impossible steep twisted stair my heart

thought it could have small uncurtained windows it could go on
being there under its tiles for the swallows
every year

love was already living in the house my heart

thought when we got there it thought it was
a letterbox a back door opening to
a garden it could walk in

it was nothing we had put there but before us it was

apple willow and a wilderness of
rose thorn thick and dark
and light with its daylong delicate flowers my heart

thought it had roots it thought it could cover its roots
with straw it thought it could carry on
lighting its every morning fire

because we as love for a while had been living there

New Year 1987

Brancaster   last bare light of the afternoon   the two of
us   that lonely ark   the sun
going down

beyond Hunstanton   where the sea   the growing dark of
us   was breaking and   I knew not how   would break
me to the bone

and long before the Romans   we walked on   the dip and shallow of
the afternoon abandoned
towards

Holkham   and before that bay   the sandbank and the half black
hulk of the wrecked ship   hope   that iron heart   how
I'd hanker after it

Love

Loneliness, learning to do up her laces early, little knows
that love is, even now, about
to kill her.

Love plucks chickens.
Love plaits with skill its black rope of hair.
Like a Chinese grandmother. Look.

Love is a bound foot. How can it learn to walk
in a landscape without hope
like the Gobi Desert?

Love is arthritic and looks as if it would like
to strangle her. Love says:
'I would like to strangle you.

It is only a joke.'
Loneliness does up her shoes with a neat double knot.
Love is a wishbone, stuck, in her throat.

The Unmaking

Old is this earthen room; it eats at my heart.
ANON

What if, in mourning, I – ?

The mountain knows me as I am unknowing
stone of its stone.

My capable uncomprehending hands.

And if sack cloth astounds me?

I could not imagine that
queer quiet queen, my heart, her earthen room.

What if, without understanding – ?

My mind, its glass bead game, its quick bright imitation
stone

and I, for its glistering –

What if the mountain, my unmaking, is?

Blackthorn

I like to imagine
the stars are something other than sewing-machines.

I am rooted, remote.

I guard the white embroidered whirlpools
of the wind.

Beyond the muted talk of angels there are quick black holes
like poems. In my heart

I hear the creak and shuttle of the earth's old bones,
the toil and spin.

I am the wake, the needle and the well
of wondering.

North

Who can refuse to live (her) own life?
ANNA AKHMATOVA

I have a new river now.

Not yours, Anna, but nearer
your Neva, nearer.

New streets, now, Newcastle
still without trees.

It has hills and wind.

Shall I find my feet that love me? Shall I
refuse them?

See, I have come without shoes.

The hills talk lightly here of built ships. Little is left
me now, a bit of walking.

About Benwell

Perhaps there will always be yellow buses
passing and Presto's
and people with faces like broken promises

and shops full of stotties and butties and buckets and bubble bath
and bones for broth
where the poor may inherit the earth

and women who will
wade into the wind and waste with hope eternal
and kids like saplings planted by the Council

and William Armstrong's endless line
of bairns, whose names, in sandstone,
rehabilitate their streets of rag and bone

where bits of paper, bottle tops and Pepsi cans blow up and down
despondently, like souls on their own.
Perhaps there will always be unremembered men

and maps of Old Dunston and Metroland and the rough blown rain
and the riding down of the sun
towards Blaydon.

After The Blaydon Races

Look how the big yellow bus of the sun bowls breakneck into Benwell also.

Shall it not, for a while, be still, with its wheel flown off?

Shall the old yellow bus, October, stop and beautifully steep us
in its pennyworth of ale, its picnic

cloth of gold unfolded on the rough grass?

Look how it briskly bowls by the rough sky-grass where houses were
and the forgotten, poor, affectionate people are,

berates us not as does the law in its bald helicopter

but, like that ribald bus on its breakneck way to Blaydon,
braves us, hedging bets

before our houses, waving, wild at heart and unrepentant
as the river, with its staithes and bridges.

Portrait of a Poet in the Kitchen

Anna Akhmatova, home of my barely constituted home, may I,

out of my sleepless nights, make yours, adoptive godmother,
all that I have and have not been and my hands making
salt pea soup, a poem.

May I commend to you all my already imagined murders
and my table.

Like her, you are here in your eyes. A thousand and one
mirrors remember now and the way the Neva flows
austerely.

Scoured is the soul's belonging.

By the uncurtained window may I remind you of, in their making
now, my spared, unsparing hills.

Clara Street

Many small stones are the sea's washboard.

Light on the step.

In the bare room, sleep.

On the windy street Polly makes her complaint.
I'll miss her

and the hills. I went to them on my bicycle
but they have no thoughts.

Love cannot be called. It comes
into leaf like the clematis by the yellow wall.

The river's a common language

and the lit stones of the yard
attentive.

Polly talks of little but.
Life is hard.

Many are the unprepared cathedrals of my heart.

Backyard

Soul in the warm bean light
of the afternoon

be, without wings, a hanging-basket
or a water-butt

and pot-whole to the wild seed-hoard
that waits.

For the porcelain moon is broken into
shards,

the heart's
small skull-plates

open.

Knock

If love took a lick at my red lion door
I'd lope off with it

to the lyke-wake of the hills,
my learnéd animals.

If love, like a wingbone, lay within me
I'd be quiet.

I'd bear with it,
the shoulderblade of bird or angel

broken in me,
anchoring.

Lord of my own heart's opening, guarded, lonely
lord, lend me

the lion and the ladybird light
of your being,

that I, in my loping and aching, might
look to it.

At the writing table

Her letter lies among those I have not yet been able to read.
She will write to me of Leningrad.

My shoulders would like to hide.

But the lamp with its blue shade loves me.
It is so irreparably still around it...

My shoulders would like not to be so broad

and the table not bare
of all but the razor-shell the North Sea laid at my door

last year. It is empty, half-open and whole.

My shoulders, irreparably
my own.

Shall I be able, still?

Letter to

Lend me four pieces of yellow paper for my delight.

Beautiful are your feet with shoes and they shall enrol
themselves in my most intimate thought.

Of the metaphysical waters of Tyne and of the hills
I shall think,

of my elliptical heart, of the moonlight
speaking with tongues.

Let me have pale yellow paper.

Let the soles of your feet leap up from it quickly.

Let there be something of bird and Bible
about your feet

and of their unbelonging. What shall I write?

There are the hills. There are black holes. There are a hundred
miles of solitude.

The waters of Tyne shall listen
to the moon-tongue

in my heart also. Let Solomon speak of festivals
of yellow paper

and of your feet, without shoes, for my delight.

Sunart

I remember the little disturbances of stone
our feet made there –

the call of the oyster-catchers
further along the shore –

the occasional car.
And if we were

careful, among the loch's accumulation of blue hills,
neither to close the soul completely

nor to break, by opening, that frail ligament
between the two halves of the ark

of any shell –
what were we listening for

as we held, still, the tiny wendletrap of April
in our cold wet hands?

A difficult hour. I remember the light
rain came out of nowhere, silently

the salt on my lips
was there.

Lighthouse, Ardnamurchan, Argyll

Bearable is the black ash bud.
Bearable, too, the bleak upland, the beautiful
abortive thorn.

But here, the word's made stone.

The earth comes to itself and is and always
shall have been.

Here, almost unendurably, I am.

In this belonging's nothing but
the wind, the wild
Atlantic.

Salt rain blinds the skin.

What's Elsinore – ?

The unimaginable log-book of the lighthouse keeper
gone.

A stubborn low house still stands,
the old sheep-pens, lashed
walls of stone.

The Swastika Spoon

Because from the bathroom window he saw the Crystal Palace burn.

Because the war did happen.

My father came home from the burning of Belsen

with bits of it under his skin and the bowl of his heart in his hands

that would never be the same again, not ever his own again.

Because of that burning down.

And, in his pocket, proudly, the souvenir spoon.

Of light tin, slowly the bowl of it has worn down.

Barely is it a spoon.

The best of my life has been stirring the Bisto in.

And was Jerusalem.

Because.

Of my father in me there has been no burning down.

In 1945

My father sat down where Belsen had been
and no birds came.

He could not listen any more.

Later the roots and stars would bring him a daughter.

They'd try to hurt him through her
singing.

He'd make her a home, he'd tell her
'Old Macdonald had a farm'

but he'd never hear again.

His ears were clogged wells. Hart's tongue
covered them.

His legs lay dying of typhus and rags.

His heart was a burnt-out chapel.

All the old hymns dried up in him like lentils.

His shoulders bore with him. Because of the farm
before the war

he'd spare his Uncle Tom.

My father sat down where butter and eggs had been
laid out.

It was in a Dutch kitchen.

The stars shone down like bits of shrapnel.

Scrub as he would, his hands would not
come clean.

Bone Note

> *The makar's wierd is to be a wanderer.*
> 'WIDSITH'

For you and the sea I would have stayed in Brighton.
Twenty years on

what you knew then wakes up in me.
I remember the story:

a boy growing up in a small Welsh working class town
picked up the violin

to play for the earliest silent films
for bread, jam.

At forty or so, in London then, you found the courage to unlearn
the old tune,

all you'd ever known,
to discipline your bones for Bach or Beethoven.

Heifetz you gave me, who, all on his own
played Bach, abruptly: sonatas, partitas for one violin.

I have nothing to play the records on.
I know them now. They are my own

uncelebrated solitude.
'This is a pleasure the man in the street knows nothing about,' you said,

and still you were not an elite.
You had learned to be quiet. You knew that

the soul has to find its own weird
way in the world. That old violin I laid

aside, when I left home.
Yet it can ache, it is my left arm's

loneliness, my fingers don't forget, my ear knows when the note
is out

and, as I learn to make my own tune
awkwardly, for discipline

I thank you and for solitude,
for what is hard,

for what, beyond the word,
begins in me and is bone-heard.

Saturnian

How much they matter, your stars, Mandelstam,
in the bare room where I write
behind hundred year old windows
all night.

What a god of lead the soul can be
in its silver lining.
Only the one word in the one constellation of words
will do for its shining.

Thomas Eckland

Tom to my sister and those few others who know me well. Used to living
deep inland, among small hills.
My sister keeps house.
We're cold and close. Sometimes I think the sea must sound
like the wind in the trees in the field
when it breaks loose.
No, I've no wife.
Master, they call me, because in my way I'm learned enough.
A dour and decorative word is God,
a spiralling road.
Myself. Stone-cutter. Occasional headstone.
Dry stone walls by trade.

Jehax

Mostly they were afraid of me.

I was tall and dark. Blue-black. I admired the moon
in my skin.

And mostly I was a king, though I was not
the son of a king. The old king
had no son.

Some trials were held to find who should succeed him.

I was fourteen when I climbed up on the Royal Stone
for the first time, felt it
foot me.

I'd outdone the others with my sling,
the small blue stone
I flung.

When I was a man, I thought my soul lived in that stone.

Now I know.

The stone lived with me
in a little bag of lion-skin,
afterwards

was hidden in the heart-roots of the unimaginable forest.

It was not passed on.

They thought my power was great.
And when I was a young man, so did I,
but I grew out of it.

Always my heart knew better.

My heart was a small wise animal within me.

To the Royal Stone they would come from world without end
to probe the sand,
mostly asking

me to make the rain –

for we were dying and our ancestors were dying too.
My heart would cry within me
for it knew.

Rain was the name of one of our gods. It came when it would.

Still I presided at the rituals
where smaller lighter men broke sacred vessels
in the sand.

We thought the unimaginable trees could ask for us as well.

And sometimes rain would come. But then

my long-deserted people let not go their thought
that I alone –

or that perhaps the sling-stone –

that within –

Maybe we thought –

Sometimes I think it did work like that.

Oboth

Utha was my wife. She howled as I left her.
She flung herself to the floor of the hut.
Packed earth it was and ashes.
I saw two little ridges of earth where she'd
dug her wooden boots in. Writhed and howled, she did.
No one was there, though they are with her now.
They are combing her hair down her back.

I am sad I had to leave my boots behind.
They'd cut them from me months before I left
because I could no longer walk but lay on the shelf
of the bed cut into the white wall by the stove.
I would not let my split boots out of my sight.
They sat side by side on the stool
and Utha did not sit on it.

I did not know my feet. I think they were white
but I felt nothing. And they did not know themselves.
Utha wrapped them in brown cloth.
She said it was an old chemise.
What is chemise? Chemise came with her
from the small town where she'd been a girl.
Chemise was before I knew her.

Forest was what we knew together. What was ours.
Edge of forest. That at our backs and before us
taiga, scrub, the coarse yellow flowers.
Carts coming over the rutted plain.
Carts that stumbled, stayed one night
then left at dawn loaded with logs of pine.
That was in summer. The short light months.

In winter, snow. Moon light of snow my boots loved.
How they let themselves in for it and were glad.
They shaped themselves to snow and me,
the hard ground that they knew.
Irith had to split them from me
with his heart-axe. Little axe
he had, tucked in his belt.

We'd sawn together and our lives were long.
It is quite hard to explain how, with each pine,
we'd come to it and known.
The first and last and inner ring.
How Irith, axe in hand, had quickly cut the tree
and how, because he was a kind man,
Irith came to cut my boots from me that day.

Lenten

He bare him up, he bare him down,
He bare him into an orchard brown.
CORPUS CHRISTI CAROL

Browses the bald head of the theologian, Beldever.
The boy plays in the dead leaves in the wood.
The oak bears up, with its leaves and buds, all winter.
Now the librarian nods.
Outside, they are cutting the tree for the cross.
By sundown it is roughly shapen.
Their curses have wakened the boy out of his dead wood,
who comes running with acorns.
The pen-handle Beldever holds in his thick and delicate hand
is made of horn.
There's hart's-tongue grown in the old well-hole in the yard.
The monks have lowered their tone.
The librarian passes, the dream of the rood in his head.
But for the blackthorn, this year, Beldever would have wed his Lord,
they've said. Down in the village
the boy has said it. Beldever – Old Bede – 's not dead.
And the crossed wood shall be borne –
from now, two Fridays – to the knoll
above the brown and budded orchard
where the boy lies buried.
And the monks shall walk with it
in the dark April day.

Preparing the Icon

Andrej Rublev (c.1370–c.1430) instructs his apprentices

Do not imagine, now, the austere sad face of John.
Before the snow falls, go to the forest.
Bring wood for the board. For days, while the stove remains
unlit in the studio, work that wood with chisel and plane
until it is smooth.
Break the ice on the water-butt then.
Prepare and apply to the board the first thin layer of gypsum
like a skin. Stretch the canvas. Then put on
a second layer of gypsum. When it is hard and dry, like bone,
rub it down till your shoulders are tired.
Draw the outline of John from the book of tracings,
the Authorised Version.
Begin your illumination with the background. Green.
Bring a bowl of eggs from the monastery farm.
Let him come loud and clear as a locust in your listening
to his God, ours. Break the eggs.
Use only the yolk for the dilution of your colours.
In the silence of falling snow and of the imagination's
cold dark halls, you'll know your own
austerity and John's.

At the Bellmaking

There was ice in the bowl
by the well

but with bread in his pocket
he went

out into the bone-blue dawn. Without
his father he went

through the thick unbearable
wood

till he came to the place where the dark had been
cleared

and where

all night in prayer

the monk had been making his big copper bell
with fire.

He thought he would wait while
he ate his bread

and when he was old, he told himself,
he would go.

*

The monk had nothing to do but blow
on his hands

for a while. The bell, in its great round
mould in the earth, was making. The child watched,

worried for him, as the man tried
not to forget

that mine of quiet
in the bone

he had made of listening
to God.

The monk tried not to imagine the big reverberations of
the bell

that would break like water over
the old stone

walls
of the monastery

but to listen now to the little bright tongues of
the earth that would tell

him the sun was about to break over
the hill

and to the silent tongue of the bell
in its making.

Mute, white must be
the heat

for the bell
to fire

whole and frail and beautiful as bone
or prayer.

*

The child watched the thin monk walking and thought
of the swan's bone

he had found that summer
when he was seven

and had thought fit
to be a soul-boat sailing along in the early morning. The sun

came over the hill.
The swan's

bone must be able to fly on its own,
must remember how

flying went, because it had been
part of a swan. The child had seen

the wild swan swinging over
the Russian plain.

The old jeweller speaks

My soul's hands were the strongest and most skilful
hands I had. At last my own

hands understood and ordered stones

from out the pits and bolt-holes of the earth. The dour

light hid, like loneliness, in them.

My own hands hobbled it. My soul's hands held

the fire and reservoir of it

until

the earth's heart beat
in every jewel

I made,

in every stone the word
was audible.

Fever Hospital, London, 1929
(for my mother)

Even the stars stop still in their indescribable spaces
to hear how it was to have scarlet fever
at five-and-a-half. They light up, listen, as you tell how,
alone, out of the universe, your mother came on a bus
and a train and a bus from Forest Hill to Tottenham
with a little case and how
in the little case there was always
a book, a couple of buns and a bit of knitting begun
for you. It was love, but you don't say so, because you're telling how
the too young nurses put you in black stockings, black boots
and a pale pink dress and sat
you on damp grass in the hospital garden and how,
because it was only April, you, at only five-and-a-half
got kidney trouble. Even the stars smile
as you tell of the specimens heated on Bunsen burners on a table
in the middle of the ward and tell how you taught yourself to read
because you were bored and how that was all
and how you yourself went back with your mother to Forest Hill.
How hopeful the stars are as they go off smoking because it is
all so incomprehensible.

My Cross

Great Aunt Agnes, with whose saintly name
Very little indeed will rhyme,
Gave me at my cavernous cold-water Christening
An appropriate gold cross but later on when no one was listening
Led me very secretly to understand that my cross was no ordinary Christian
Thing I must bear, but one pagan, strange and in fact Egyptian:
An ankh
For which I must thank
Her and the Lady with whom she travelled all about the earth
Being a Lady's maid in her narrow ship's berth.
I do thank her
For this rose-engravéd anchor
Which, when my soul-boat is all battered and adrift
On the unfathomable seas, finds a tiny cleft
Like the one in Rock-of-Ages-cleft-for-me
And fixes itself in there strongly
And makes an inviolable rocking home
Of my soul-boat until the seas are good and calm.
Ankh means life, says my Concise Oxford Dictionary
And I wonder why there is as yet no Insurance Company
With such a sturdy helpful name.
Perhaps I will start one. Great Aunt Agnes used to comb
My unholy difficult hair
Saying what-lovely-curls until I would have hit her
Except she always gave me a threepenny bit for my tin bank
With which I intend to start an Insurance Company called Ankh.

Cam

Always I'd one leg longer than the other.
I wrote seven letters to Camaria.
I sewed twelve handkerchiefs of fine blue linen for her.
'Lame' couldn't stop me leaping up at her.
I loved her in the cradle of the stars
and in the chair.
Camaria: 'the sea comes to'.
I could never not hear it at the night door.

The cow's bell coming slowly
from among the trees, the byre below
the small house on the hill's quiet side.
A lifetime's listening for.
The sour bread rising by the fire.
I'd walk before the dark
the day comes to.
My short leg strove.
I saw the little colours of lichen.
Sometimes I thought my longer leg would like
to walk further, alone.
I'd gather berries for the big blue bowl.
Some I washed for myself and some, carefully, for Camaria.

Morne

Morne was my name and the name of the mountain.

Cold moon, crossing the doorstone, came
in a dream of her then. I knew

my mother. Kettle and spoon could not.

Self a dark stone. I, seven. Took Morne
to the mountain. Set her down.

Tamora, the mountain

I left her there among the plantain and the stones.

The lizard came to inspect her with its tongue.

Cloud-shadows separated in their passing
over her. The stars stood

guardedly. The bare rock burned.

Tamora, tongue of stone.

Her telling, blown like sand, inherits nothing.

Only the bones of the girl I laid upon her
shall be quick with her

bare knowing.

Egrit

Egrit, old by then.
A leg I'd never loved was gone.
I walked with a stave of thorn,
proud of my understanding.

Tales were told in the hall.
I knew them as I knew the land,
its old light hills.
I did not listen when they talked of miracles.

As if the child could live and die again.
We'd set a stone.
I knew I'd not walk properly again
and I'd the vegetables.

Women without children, wild and thin
and clothed in brown.
Nothing about them
but walking. In my bones

I felt for them and further on,
where the old road makes an unexpected turn,
they sat down.
Slept.

One set her staff beside her
in the ground. It, while she slept, took root,
as if it woke, was
budded. They walked on. And then

we'd a tree of our own
and such and such a one already cured,
they said. An odd word,
miracle.

I looked to my own stave.
Thorn. I thought it would not,
when the wild March wind came on,
flower white again.

Nailish

My name meant crippled.

Stood, like God the Mother, on its sudden hill
our ordinary, extraordinary cathedral.

Swallows were like small dark angels
there, they said

and I could well imagine.
When from my narrow bed I heard the bells

my heart remembered that

the moon was like a small bent needle and my spine
was black.

But Julian would wash her hands of that and without haste or hark-back
would make well my walking

and my wasted leg,
my will. In that midsummer of my thought

the light was like skimmed milk.

Mary

They will say that I kept all these things in my heart
and pondered them.

They will write it down.
I'll forget

how I fought imagination. Was it my own
indisputable angel?

Shortly they'll say that God sent Gabriel. That's what
they'll write. And what

is Gabriel but the word for morning? Light
of the orange-blossom.

I'll remember the road to Bethlehem. How we said nothing.
I shall return

to be one who will gather the stars like volcanic stones
in her apron.

Conventual

For God in me had shoulders of warped wood
and was a well

made ill with holy water.

Like the bitter withy God in me was thin, a broken
spine, a broken

violin, a whole ship
burial

of sound. God was the excommunicated wind
and crooked as a thorn

or gargoyle. God had a withered hand, a tongue of wood
like half a castanet

and could no longer set a keel
of thought

upon the water at Monkwearmouth
as in Bede he could.

Camaria

I

The coral reefs are derelict cathedrals and the sea-grass
is no longer singing.

Of the fixed and wandering angels, who can tell? Each one's mislaid
itself. Each one's

a lost tongue or a lout.

Despair lies thick upon the waters, thick as dust
or sleep.

And of Camaria? Whose soul elaborates the sea's
caught up in it.

II

Dust does not dream of itself. Nor does it
doubt.

The beautiful reverberations of the bell are daunted.

This is the sleep of louts.

III

Camaria comes as sea-cow or the moon's clay
light.

She looks, from her rock, at the delicate water, ill
as the laughter of mislaid angels, quiet
as the bell.

Ereshkigal in the Rocking-Chair

I am resplendent here in the sacred rocking-chair of your heart.
I'll not put off the stained and tattered black I wore,
the rut and dirt, the roads I walked. Barefoot
I've broken stones for bread. And now I'll sit as cast
clout to the clean and upright rocking-chair you christened
Abraham. No more will I break the stem of Jesse
or my old clay pipe for him. I'll smoke tobacco
for the black madonna of my own delight. For I am
queen of the mystic, desolate night and of the solitary
moon. And you, on this mid-November afternoon
of mist and thought, would claim me as your own?
Then bring me the nuns, that demolition gang of wooden women.
Bring me the girl you were, the virgin Mary with her
sleeves on fire. Bring me your black and tattered
academic gown, your God, the literary men
and women you have loved and all
your little revolutions.

from

NANTUCKET AND
THE ANGEL

(1997)

the saints set off without their woolly vests
the little saints set off into the snow
they leave behind their hagiographies
but humbly take their shoes
for they have many miles to go
and versts and versts of Russian snow
engulf the sickle and the plough

The Singing Pylons

Glumdalclitch, glumdalclitch, glumdalclitch
They mumble on dark summer days. They say *Tch tch*
To the muddle of low-flying larks, bees, gnats and, later on, bat-
Mobiles caught by the light
Of the moon in the pliant wire. *Tch tch*
Grumble these Big Friendly Giants on crutches.
And we who've no share in the profit and loss of it all
Also grumble. For having to live with them makes us ill –
And who's cut an oblong hole in the wood
To make them a road –
And look at the laidly worm of the wire that lollops o'er hill and dale
We say, becoming lyrical
In the midst of our dry ecological battles
Remembering *Palgrave's Golden Treasury* and school.
But here comes a candle to light us to bed.
Here comes a big trade
Wind that would tear not only a land but an ozone layer to tatters –
And what does it matter
Then? For then they sing their one peculiarly lovely tone
Across these half-forgotten
Northern hills. O all night long they sing
Their lonely song, like whales uninterrupted, to Esh Winning
And, if they could, they'd sit down
And weep by the waters of Wear or Babylon
For they are exiles. Lashed in a land of blown plastic bags
They're longing for Brobdingnag.

Volcano

Vindolanda. Wind-land. Bare
Outland of bone and unbeliever.
Longing in the long alone of wall for world's end.
Cloud accumulates and we are not
At one with the beyond. Sicilian sun
Now nothing but apricot, Etna and that
Old palaver in the olive grove.

Fenlight

Alan of Walsingham, Sacrist, practical man –
quo se verteret vel quid ageret,
not knowing which way to turn nor what to do –
knows vertigo –
as if the Isle of Ely had gone down
into the fen –
as if his spine were broken – knows
he must invent the earth again and God
and therefore send to Stamford
for new stone.

His job is to imagine, to administrate
materials and men. His mind's
dismantled. First he's only able to invent the erstwhile –
transept, chancel, nave – not
penetrate the unimaginable
hole where –
quo se verteret vel quid ageret –
the ordinary fenlight enters and it feels
as if the sparrows flying in and out
are flying in his heart.

His job's to order men and boats to bring out more
of that once wholly to be trusted
Barnack stone
and build again –
but he is momentarily unsure.

My heart unsettled

Harriet Traherne was here one hundred years ago. I hear
her treadle still.
The dead lie naked on the battlefield.
Edgehill.

Half lovely is the little morning light
in patches.
I have brought Harriet's sleeve to gather
in running stitches.

The flags are cold beneath the new fen rushes
we laid yesterday.
Harriet's Bible, dried flowers, needles
will be safe with me.

And here's her clasp of gold that grips my skull,
its amethyst.
The dead are only hidden
by the mist

that rises from the battlefield, the horses gone. I hear
the lap and tap
of winter jasmine at the window
and the leap

of flame. And Harriet Traherne's at home with her
metallic smell
of scissors and the lame sound of her
treadle.

From the diary of Hannah Bishop, Holbeck House, Ely, 26 October 1642

On hesitating to depict my grandmother

She must have alighted like a bird
into Bertha Elizabeth,
being, the fourth
of John King, Gentleman, late of Hartest, hard

by Sudbury. Late of London, now, her body lies
alone, eludes me, bone of her
impenetrable bone. Her
soul – I wouldn't sentimentalise.

Her stone's among the stones
of gentlemen within the wall, the toll
of bell, bird-chortle.
But she's flown.

Delta
(for my grandmother)

The summer that I was departing, departing for ever
in small boats down the Danube delta
ducking mosquito-nets
she died.
Every afternoon she died in Dorking
being all bone, done in.
Where was I, called for, ever again, being gone?
I was gadding about in foreign
boats. Still, more or less, unbitten, blue-eyed
and rowed
among reeds, I gazed for the first time on Russia, land-
fall of longing, forbidden, beyond.
And when they drew the curtains round her bed
I was sleeping it off in Belgrade –
that early rising, daily, in the delta, from the white mosquito-cloth.
And did she know death
as the awful effortless rowing toward
among thick reed-beds?
Did she take hold of the oar in both hands?
I did, before leaving that waterland
to go back to Belgrade.
But Dickie, where's Dickie? she said.

The Garden in Esh Winning

Go then into the unfabricated dark
With your four bare crooked tines, fork,
And get my grandmother out of that muddle of dock and dandelion root
And put an end to neglect
While the wind says only *Esh Esh*
In the late apple blossom, in the ash
And all the hills rush down to Durham
Where the petulant prince bishops dream
In purple vaults.
It's not the earth's fault,
Fork, but mine, that I for forty years of days and nights invented dragons
To guard my grandmother's bare arthritic bones
From my own finding. Now of all things I imagine a garden
Laid over, and dumb as, a disused coalmine.

In the north there are no salley gardens, no, nor bits of willow pattern
Plate to plead for me, no, only bones
Unmourned, the memory of the memory of a plane shot down
And its discolouration.
Who now humbly brings me my grandmother in pieces
Like Osiris,
Fork? Who eases out old sorrel gone to seed, old scallions?
Who pulls the purple columbines
Out of the not quite dark midsummer midnight? In the north the sky is green,
The long grass, partly shorn, lies down like a lion
And *something's happened to John*
And in this valley of discoloured bones
Ezekiel lies open to the wind, the fork-work done.
The Bible propped like an elbow on the ironing-board within
The house is full of visions, Gran,
Of what we are, were, always might have been.

On reading Walter de la Mare's *Come Hither* in 1994

When I was a swanlake girl, with oars, my grandmother was with me in
        the boat
And she, before her final stroke, was fat,
Being full of bread and butter and brazil nuts.

There was, I found out, a hole in her heart –
In the fuselage of her heart – that one dark night
In the war the fire had gone out.

Both weight and measure was my grandmother, my dear dour ballast,
With her *Lest*
We all forget. The blasted stars I had to steer by –

I was afraid they'd go entirely
Out or turn out
To be nothing but brazil nut

Shells. I wonder over Walter de la Mare's
Come Hither. Forty years
Too late, I understand

How we were driven by the night wind
In her heart, how it
Made dry land of our dreams, a veritable desert,

How it brought our little boat about, about
And roundabout.

O brave new world, that was, that had such girlhood in it.

Fantasia
(i.m. Anna Slawinska, 1900-1921)

Her last September and the wind was in the larch beyond
the summerhouse, the long bay window, where we sat and
sorted lavender for hours, for little pillows.

That was what we did those slow September days.
Karelia: our slipshod grandmother and Anna and myself.

Anna brought me chocolate widows from St Petersburg.
They must have been the last before the Revolution
put an end to them for ever. *Mesdames Morozowa,
Old Believers*: so we named them, nibbling and beheading.

Scarves, shawls, aprons, sweet felt boots: so the widows went.

And Anna in her old blue dress she called *Neva*. Anna bent
embroidering the three silk pears she had begun

for Nana Poliowska,
for our mother, newly dead, who would be lost without us,
for myself, her Unlamented, as she said.

Stuffed pears, their silk already faded: old rose, sage and grey
as the weathered boards of the summerhouse. *As the old felt
boots of the grandmother* said Anna over my shoulder.
She was fond of Nana Poliowska.

Then Anna dead. Dead as a chocolate widow. In October.
Nana Poliowska involved elsewhere –

in flannel and goose grease and *pâté de foie gras* and
in her old Karelia, the light snow-wind and prayer.

Wanda Slawinska, Paris, 1951

On being the littlest Russian nest egg doll

I hear hearts beating round me, four or five of them, like drums
we are inside. We are immortal. We are wood.

I hear the soft wood-fibre settle into knots.

I hear the plot and fidget and the rote
of Masha, Masha.

We are all called Masha.

I hear the first five notes of song that Noah's wife took with her
when the waters broke, about

the Volga boatmen. Now I hear the shouts.

Deaf Fishergirl

It's complicated, like the inside of my brother's boat.
Sound breaks off abruptly at the edge of me.
The world stops short. The sea frets
stone. It frets and laps the step where I stand waiting
for my brother's boat. I think the sea turns
everything to sand. Its salt eats wood and thought.
But laughter is a spiral and the path that climbs the hill
in Bible pictures and the brittle empty basket
waiting with me. Laughter's coiled and cooped like rope.
In cottages and in the smoke-house it is clammy. Here
the air caresses me or cuts me to the quick. And clouds come
from the edge of sea one day, the edge of hills another,
or they come in with the nets. And once
when I was seven I was listening to the light on water, listening
to the sparkle of the light on stones
and waiting for my brother.

The Death of Pietro Faldi

Pietro taught me to listen. Sometimes he stood on his head
but the lesson was always the same. It was old
as the earth by then. His learned hand and shoulder listened to
the violin, the still leaping bow.
He didn't always hear me when I spoke to him.
He touched my wrists lightly, to loosen them.
And then the boy brought me the loosened bow.
There were no more lessons.

My erect head listens secretly.
My brothers and sisters sit upright at table.
We all do. There are no differences between us.
The cutlery shines on the polished mahogany board.
We wait for my father to come from the library.
Water shines in the finger-bowls.

There is a loneliness that one dismisses easily.
One tightens the bow. One tunes.
One turns the pegs – it is always awkward.
Suddenly the shoulders want to fly away.

Princesse de la Maison d'Este
(after the 15th century portrait by Pisanello)

After Vermeer's 'Lady and her Maid-servant'

– O yes, I'd forgotten that, the rabbit-catcher's bill.
Separate from the meat, that's the trouble.
I always forget to include it.
Stop the rabbit.
– Yes, Madam.
There is no door beyond them,
Only the dark, immeasurable, the dark
They must have gone into, doubting the polished ark,
Its full pepper pot, its perfectly done accounts
And only the small belated entry of the rabbit
Letting the laughter of the soul
Be heard at all.

After Breakfast

She hears the little thud of angels coming to.

She smells their pomegranate smell.

She smiles.

The bowls go round and round like other worlds or rowing-boats
below the weir

where she, without oars in the rocking-chair, can hear the angels
come and go

between the kettle and the fire. She feels the flood
of folded wings,

the pelt
of

purple shadows settle on her
shoulders

like a shawl.

NANTUCKET AND THE ANGEL
Sketches

(for Margaret Wilkinson)

Rocking-chair

Nantucket's not a bit like Rembrandt's mother reading.

She's a riot and a reverence of thought, apparent
quiet, espresso, coffee pot.
                                    For if
you left her rolling cigarettes, she'd like as not
set fire to all the rocking-chairs
wherein she ever sat.
                            If not, she'd chafe and suffer
long, as T.S. Eliot, years after *Four Quartets*, sat chewing sweets

and all the little bits of laughter left in her
would sail out like a fleet of fishing-boats
upon the hill she looks at.
                                    She's set fair
to, what d'you call it, meditate or make up hats and pockets
for the angels hitherto unheard,
unheard of.
                    Fierce, the far, fetched light she fettles by,
would get her bread by, knitting, if
her fingers would.

Phoenix

She's both axe and off-cut.
                                    Come now, cross-examine her
with grace and fervour.
                            Is she not also her grandmother's
tacked-together pocket, pre-war blanket with watermark,
tarnished brass tap, broken cup, phoenix
with terribly singed wing-tip?

                    Don't expect her
to have got the act of mutability together yet,
at ninety, with a name like that, Nantucket,
cloistered, clobbered with annunciation.
                              Is she, like
Isak Dinesen back in Denmark, living on oysters, champagne?
Absolutely not.
                    With Nantucket it's Guinness and milk.
Polly put her onto it.

Narrowboat

Admit she's not Elijah,
cheer

the rocking-chair that isn't chariot?
Nantucket

moors, long past midsummer.
Long past war

she listens to the star
light, loud as colliery choirs.

Nantucket, narrowboat, steers
not by stars

but by her angel Gabriel's pocket silver
pig of pure

annunciation plots her course. Her bones are brittle,
curses, trombones, break. As well

she might break herself in
for heaven.

Niche

Nine little drawers of nails. Like sins
she has scrubbed them under the niche in the scullery wall.
They are beautiful, secular nails.
They're for pinning the angel to his pedestal,
for his beatitude, her latitude, her
collection of Lepidoptera.
She pretends he's a cabbage white butterfly.
He's put in his place anyway.
He is her museum piece.
He is a perpetual reminder of her miserliness.
His love for her soul is inconsequential, she says.
There is dust in his pocket.
He is no longer numinous.
But lovely nails. She licks them clean
like Charlie Chaplin.

Ocarina

For Chinese duck feathers make a shambles.
For she shakes her pillow at the hill-sheep opposite.
All we like sheep have gone astray she notes *except for me and Isaiah.*
For the angel hovers at the window with her.
For he empties the best brass ashtray.
For he has patted the dust out of his particular cushion, the embroidered one,
    obediently.
For he has been rolling small French cigarettes for her.
For he has become her consort.
For he has laid down his ocarina for her.
For he has folded his wings like sails or flanelette sheets.
For he would surround her with his wings in all weathers, but he is ashamed
    of them.
For their seams have become crooked.
For not even the attic can accommodate wings which open like windows.
For shut, they have become arthritic.
For cat-fleas sit and sing in the interstices of their splendid scales.
For these are finer than flanelette, actually more like fish-gills.
For he is afraid of the crows that come into the garden for pieces of stale scone.
For she has taught him to say scone like her Suffolk godmother, Phyllis.
Stone the crows he says.

Pistachio

For her he splits pistachios and cardamoms with care,
with thoughtful, long thumbnail. Nantucket idles, nods, admires.
For hours she'll sit and trace the dead bits in the Tradescantia.
He'll fetch the mat but fail to meditate on candlestick or pewter
coffee-pot. He wants his ocarina back. He's lachrymose, laconic,
carves *Nantucket* into Lipsalve, bootblack, Vick.
Painstakingly he'll learn to spell *pistachio* and *Pelargonium*. He'll
even open mange-touts with his long thumbnail.

Mud

She gets wet washing the elephant under the alder.
She has erected nets around it and the endless river.
She has removed her shoes because they are sacred.
Now she remembers, she's painting the elephant blue.
Great Aunt Adelaide! she says aloud.
The charabanc's bent beneath the weight of woad.
She is light as a farthingale, a girl.
I recall she says.
What? says the angel.
I'll never forget that bold expedition of elders and betters
The mud on the elephant's feet in the musical garden
The meadowsweet at Wisley, Wallington
Wait she says
With a long walk back to the station
Wherever it was, white roses
She reminisces well.
But the angel is now, like a bed of nails.

Misericord

He borrows an old tweed coat with toggles.
He takes himself off to the cathedral.
He's going to look at gargoyles.
But first he kneels.
God he says *she's impenetrable.*
Someone is hoovering the carpet in the choirstalls.
There is mud there dropped from the hem of the Bishop's stole.
He imagines himself without wings wearing a torn orange overall.
He learns he has ears like wells.
Only a Tibetan or an archangel can hear a school
Of overtones take off like pterodactyls
Out of mud and misericord. *O Hell*
He says aloud. *O Hassocks* He is seasick with the lovely swell
Of sound of hoovering. He's rude and inconsolable.
The borrowed pocket turns out to be full of little
Old tobacco bits that he could sit and roll
Up in his exile.
He knows not to smoke in the cathedral.
He rips a page from out the nearest hymnal.
He's left the Rizla papers hidden underneath his pedestal.
He lights a candle for her soul.

Distraction

Once it was wood pigeons. One in particular put her out of time.
Now it's a cock that aches for it, aches for denial, with his din.
Now it is April, April original perennial as sin, the same that
With his shourès soote the droghte of March hath percèd to the roote.
And now it's him with his perpetual assumption *Nan, dear Nan*
And every evening his hand in her own.
And nextdoor's television set in fits of laughter, everlasting
Laughter, guns, the opening bars of Beethoven.
The village's only ice cream van, *The Teddy Bears' Picnic* peripatetic.
Round and round the garden of Gethsemane go they
That slepen al the nyght with open eye.
His hand in her own, like a signature tune.

Untitled

He has taken Nantucket away as if it were a ball point pen or poetry.
We don't know where she is, though so many tell us...
So Louise and Frances Norcross learned of the death of Emily Dickinson's
        mother
In a letter dated late November 1882. *She slipped from our fingers...*
I cannot tell how Eternity seems. It sweeps around me like a sea. His hand,
The angel's hand, the emptiness of love, in hers.

Rain

Nettles have renewed her hands.
They sting, like stigmata.
Now there is rain.
Not rain as Noah knew it, but enough to nobble her.
She walks among imaginary animals, the ark-stalls
Of the horse, rhinoceros and hippopotamus.
The house lists riverward.
The elephant is wet, the bright woad fades.
There's innocence abroad.
There is the special anonymity of rain.
The angel walks in wellingtons.
He opens his wings like butterflies or bi-planes out beyond the wood.
She opens her drawers of bread.
All her mistakes are laid before her.
Liberty bodices, Lepidoptera.

Table

O but they ache in her like bones.
Her trespasses, she means.
They traipse about like Israelites in Egypt.
Stick, like bits of bread unleavened, in her throat.
Trip her up like acciaccaturas, accidental notes.
Defy her like an old sum in delirium.

We do not presume to come to this thy Table, O merciful Lord...
Comfortable Words says the angel, breaking bread.
Crumbs of comfort he adds.
Sin, she decides.
Sins. Like black-eyed beans. Like Beethoven.
She is proud of her bread, proud like Emily Dickinson.
She knows the Encyclopaedia of Music inside out.
Life with you, Gabriel she says *is unnecessarily complicated.*
Like a grace note.

Ennui

There is her bleak old head bent over the book and the apple bud.
There is the woolly aphid.
There is mud.

There is the angel bedraggled by the springing briar.
There are the secateurs.
There are thickets of air.

There is the big yellow bucket of weed and wedding.
There on the hill are the wet stars wading.
There is Rembrandt's mother reading.

Eggs

The angel discovers the blackbird's nest in the cut-back clematis
Under the windowsill. A little lookout on the hill.
And of its fat brown sitting bird he is not afraid.
He begs to examine the eggs.
They are mottled brown like Nantucket's skin.
They are snug and fat, like secrets, an exact fit
In their own straw pocket. He examines them
And in the shantung pockets of his wings he aches for them.
He wants to take them home with him.
Nantucket sulks.
She tucks her elbows in.
She calls him an April fool.
She'll tell him, it's *her* April.

Chocolate

It's anyone's April, eight years after Chernobyl.
Her heart was immune to all that. It kept on
With its small dry beat like a metronome, polite
And quiet as a queue of people waiting for kelp tablets.
Later she dreamt of the ill-dressed children of Byelorussia,
The made ill children of Minsk who came to her door, who were
Pale as the seraphim –
And she with a tea-towel on her arm
Tried to comfort, to tempt them to old milk chocolate.
Later she heard of the Elephant's Foot –
Once molten, then immutable, a bit like a heart set
Down within the stone Sarcophagus at Pripyat –
And wept.

Au matin

She rises early now, like Colette's mother, among closed flowers.
The *brioche* and the Beaurepaire of the day are hers
Alone. She inspects the cloches, the ruined cathedrals
Of air between cars. What she calls
Air is gone and she must make do with imagination
Even in the morning, *au matin*.
Air, like silence, like the elephant, the old salt-lick
And promise of the earth, is gone, now Gabriel lies sick.

Scrabble

Ein jeder Engel ist schrecklich or, if you press her, *Every angel? Terrible.*
Rilke, at nobody's beck and call, alone in his airy improbable
Princess Marie von Thurn und Taxis castle,
Put it well enough. But Gabriel? *He's ill*
She'll tell you, *pale* –
And that's expensive like an Easter candle –

Prim as a pebble, can't spell
Ipecacuanha. So she'll bicker with her soul, like Babel,
Like a bag of boys at Scrabble, like eleven chickpeas on the boil
At no one's beck and call. Nantucket sets about her special awful gruel,
Her own *Duino Elegy*, her doggerel.

Gone

He's risen like the skylark from its nest of grass.
He's risen from his antic nest of illness
Awkwardly. For Gabriel has lost the knack and snare of wing,
Has risen therefore less as skylark than as man and in his going
Without gruel or grace goes to the graceful places of his own desire.
He's gone to lend the wind an ear
At dry stone walls.
He's gone to let the unattended school of hills –
The humpbacked whale and shale and vellum of them –
Sail upon him
Sitting still. He's gone to learn from lichen
Something of the scale and making of the skin.
He's gone beyond the field barn to the brown bogwater and the tarn
To sodden his shoes, to break his feet in, gone
To let the quibble of the sheep, the quiet of sheep-
Fold open sleep
In him. And well beyond the stone smallholding
He is gone, to let the affable unfolding –
Fell by fell and tale by tale, untold, star-holding – tell
Upon him and the yellow tormentil.

Everything

With handkerchiefs and tea-towels busily Nantucket boils the wings
He left behind him on the floor.
Holy-Mary-Mother-of-God! and *Men!* she says, and more.
And now that's everything.
She hangs his last two bits of linen on the line to air:

A pair of curtains, poor, embroidered, pre-war
Colliery banners, bold, queer, cumber-
Some reminders of an old crusade, cathedral-bare,
A pair of Bayeux tapestries.
So many metaphors.
She's far too old to mend them or her ways.
They are her colours and her code of honour.
Here's the elephant, she'll say
And here, with Chaucer, are the smale fowele of the air
And here am I.
For they shall be her shroud, her bottom drawer.
For now she'll do with all the dignity of widowhood
And keep the woolly aphid from the door.

Epilogue

She will get out of her godlessness again and again.
She will enter cathedrals.
She'll carry her shoes in her hand.
She will sit under the wire and wait for the swallows' return.
She'll sit under the willow and mend her old grey cardigan
With wool the colour of stone.
She will walk by water.
She will uncover the old forgotten bridlepaths, the poor
Ways of the packhorse and the pilgrim and the earth.
She will discover the mute illumination of the moon.
She'll sleep under stones: they will turn to butter or gold in the churn.
She will cross plantations.
She will no longer understand.
She will dust the ash of cigarettes and angels from her hands.
Come winter, she'll be black ash bud and bone.

*   *   *

In leafmould long

In leafmould long he's lain. Faith's
borne him

bodily. The woods fold in as I, unbound, bend over him
beneath the alder,

listening. The leaves alight. Nor is the least
sound lost in this

November wood, where, undisturbed,
God's

distances, like stars, disintegrate,
protect

heart's rooting and the new heart's
shoot.

Annunciation

What if this were the angel Gabriel? Something there

is that aches so through the soul
it accomplishes clay
and cardigan,

carries on walking down the garden, past
the old blackbird's nest, empties
the compost –

herbal teabag with its label,
eggshell, Christmas
orange peel –

composes itself like an old wives' tale. Who said there

was nothing about you
borrowed or blue
or virginal?

Epiphany

They must have known, because they were kings, they'd have to go on
collecting camel-dung.

You don't have to cross the abyss of sudden understanding.

You go on polishing brass. Maybe the toasting-fork turns
into a runcible spoon.

You go on taking down the tree's twelve days of Christmas, dust them
one by one.

You pack away the partridge Clara made of bottle corks,
become the mistress of the ark,

its candle magic. You become a thirteenth moon.

You boil the turkey-bones to make a little earth-
broth Oliver laps from the wassail-cup

as if it were water or love.

You must have known you'd go to sea in a sieve and survive.

By the time they got home, they must have known, been nearly able
to name, the neverending

world of wind, sand, dung. It must have been on the tip of the tongue.

The Garden

The stars will not applaud you. They are absorbed
in their own beatitudes

like God. You were in love with the splendid
rosewood of the Word.

And now the word *rose* weeps for you.

And now the word-hoard, gnostic, as at Nag Hammadi
knows you,

you, unlettered and alone as Mary Magdalene
or any woman

walking in a garden
wondering.

Mary Magdalene

As if the earth were lost, she finds an apple in the long, lit grass.
Now she forgets, and now laments, her tangled hair.
The old tunes are like locusts with their knotted legs.
Kumbaya, my Lord, kumbaya.
Come by the long, lit ways of the savannah.
There is silence because of the dead wasp and the spider.
Silence is not an angel. It has legs.

God's Leg
(for my father)

I made this garden for God not far from Lüneburg.
He'll walk there with his gammy leg
And not forget, for that old fool of a leg will always be in uniform.
He'll think to himself: I am, I am.
He'll think he's on top of a flame-throwing tank that's entering Belsen
Again, again.

'Stone-bald, water-subtle...'

Stone-bald, water-subtle, silent as the star-field's stubble-burning
is the soul.
Hiroshima happens, perhaps, or rosebay willowherb roots
in its navel.
If it could, I suppose, it would hope, rebel, hobble, hold out
its wooden bowl.

Armagnac

Cézanne, *sur le motif,* looked and looked at the incalculable
mountain

of his heart made motiveless
by light.

Who listens to the light in *Armagnac* may listen
to the way

it floats the heart on the incalculable
waters

like an ark, unanchored,
held

and even unto Ararat. The work's made
motiveless.

What you need to know for praying

You need to know that no one has been here before,
not even you, though you are as ever

kneeling on the oblong Indian rug, its faded
tree, its dry blue birds.

You may imagine that
they sing. You need to know that

everyone who was or is or will be's
here with you in your always

unswept room. You may imagine it's an ark, the first or last,
and that the earth spins, scattering dust.

You need to know your heart
will beat

its wings,
will not berate you for imagining

you've sent it out,
a solitary raven, on its way from Ararat.

All Shall Be Well

Julian started this or it was
that small pot
from Norwich now with its little arrangement of lungwort,
primroses

which even and all through January flowered
beneath the house wall,
Esh, the hill
and where the pit was, sheltered

as if by her hand or by the fold of her
big brown anchorite
skirt.
So I imagine, sitting here

in the sun, knowing
all shall be well
and all manner of thing shall be well,
not writing about that knowing

and all the arrangements I never made for it.

LINTEL

(2001)

On the Dark Side of the Moon

I hear the stars exploding all around me with a soft wet sound.

I hear the exasperated wind.

I hear my feet rasp. How they long to rest themselves on moss.

I hear sand turn to less

and less than itself. I hear my tongue,

stone, hollowing.

I hear the earth, a clay pot on a wheel.

I hear the soul's

song, what is near.

I hear the waterholes, the stricken cattle of the air.

The Makings of Marmalade

unripe oranges in silk-lined sacks
sow-bristle brushes
china jugs of orange-washing water
one big bowl
pith-paring knives, one for each woman
a mountain of sugar, poured slowly
a small Sevillian well
songsheets against the tedium, in parts
pine cones for burning
silver spoons for licking up the lost bits
a seven-gallon pot
a waxed circle, a sellophane circle, elastic
small pieces of toast

Scheherazade

He is languid as a fed lion.
She in her salt and sackcloth gown is gone
into a wilderness of wind at noon

where the wonderful covered well of tales
is a dry waterhole
or a bell

abandoned. What is the sound at noon
of silence in a grain
of sand? It may be what is borne

by her beyond the hollowed bone of thought,
the loud elaborated heart,
the salt

and sack-
cloth shadow begging briefly at her back,
her Bedouin back.

Sarah's Laughter

Sarah's laughter's sudden, like a hurdle, like an old loud crow
that comes out of the blue.

The graceful men at the makeshift table –
there, in the shade of the tree, in the heat of the day, in Bethel –

look up from the all too tender veal,
the buttermilk, the three small

cakes of meal she's made them. For her husband
Abraham, she's sifted, shaped them in her old dry hand.

Good Lord, no. Laugh? Not I. For Sarah's suddenly afraid.
She did what she could

when she sent him in to that Hagar, handmaid, then,
yes, then dealt hardly with her, only then

let her bide with the lad
Ishmael. A sturdy lad.

It's hidden, the hurt, like a hard little bird in the tent
of her heart. She's tended it.

To Lot's Wife

At least we don't know your name. It might have been

one that meant halt, handmaid, hard to insult
in the old Hebraic tongue.

Silt-white, anonymous, you might have been
any woman, any

one of us who, turning, turns
attention

to the bed, to linen, to belonging
bare and dear

enough to hang onto.

Look, you've already lost your daughters.

Later they'll lie with their father, their future
laid down.

Look at the city of salt and exult.

Lighter than laughter you are at the last
and alone.

Annunciation

I was alone at the well.
I was doused in shadow and in deed.
My yoke lay on the ground, waiting.
I cannot say what I mean.
I was come upon.
I was going to carry the water to my espoused man,
Joseph, of the house of David.

A Letter from Marie-Claire to Her Sister
Paris, February 1910

Now I can see the unevenness of the wall and the place
where the icon was.

She called it *La Vieille*.

Mary's dress, a greenish blue, was like the sea.

I wish I were in Dieppe, still walking on the grey sea-wall.

I wish I were in Dieppe, still counting the cobbles.

I wish I were in Dieppe, asleep with her in the low dark room,
still waiting for the boat to come.

I hear her now: *Claire, Marie-Claire,*
bring me my pearl. They buried it with her.

They buried her in the sea with its great grey swell.

When I got back here I was ill.

Guillaume's Loom, Hastings, 1080

I made a loom for Mathilda, my English daughter.
'Mathilde!' I called. I wanted to show her
The strong clay rings I'd made to hold the thread
As hard and near as I held her. I wasn't proud
Of the rest – a rough affair of stick and thole
Cut from the worst English wood, I think hazel,
And English wool.

Margaret Heslop on the morning
of her father's funeral, February 1627

I am left to winter light and the will of God
now Father is dead.
Magda, the wooden-haired doll, is with me, laid
on the windowsill in her wooden bed.
I'll take the grace and loneliness of morning with me when we go
among the dark yews to my father's burial and know
my being alone here is – well, loveliness.
Being here in my black wool dress.
Martha put the lead-weights in my hair
before she lit the fire
this morning. So it won't curl.
Those who are to come to Father's funeral
will crowd in curiously. One day
a married, meek-haired Margaret will come, a long time after me.

Her Father Walks Over Eggleston Moor

I will take her the sunlight caught in my coat, its smell of wool.
I will take her the boat-on-wheels –
I dare say Martha will be good enough to mend the smaller sail.
I will take her the sound of the sea that has crossed the hills
Without its shell.

Her Father in the Patients' Garden, Newcastle Borough Lunatic Asylum, 1919

I am not lost. I harbour my loneliness here
By the larkspur. Here, where the hand of my daughter,
Margaret's hand in hard love, took my elbow –
The smell of the ward's in my hair.
Behind me now, the black clocktower, the wall –
O God, our... God, reported missing and presumed, etcetera,
When they built that wall.
I'll take my soul and sixpence when I go.
I'll go to Muriel, though she is laid
Aside. *My mother, Dad, my mother's...* Margaret said.
The stones of the path in the patients' garden –
Narrow then wide, narrow then wide.

Carmody Visits the Lock-keeper's Daughter

Those who made lace were here before me.
My father and mother forget sometimes to walk in front of me.
Last night I heard the linnet sing
and now there is the dull canal of coming
here. I dream I bear my own black boat upon my back
and can't abandon it.
I'll buy her linen thread to caulk the seams of it.

In Old Age He Visits Eugenie's Grave

Here is the pocket in which, all my life, I have carried her
small silver casket. Here is the casket.
Look, how it catches at light, like a heart, like water.
'Ca' the Yowes' she sang to me under the alder that wet night.
She sang like Kathleen Ferrier.
There are flowers hereabout, in the mist, in the smirr.
I've brought her a basket of eyebright,
brought them from the moors.

My Camberwell Grandmother Before Her Marriage

The upholsterer's late.
He'll say that he couldn't get over the road at New Cross Gate.
A little man from Mile End, moth-eaten.
Must have grown up on bread and gin.
How did Father get hold of him? I don't know.
I wish he had not. For now
There's no end to the mending of Mother's old chairs, the ones
She chose from Dickens and Jones.
I wish she'd gone out of this life
Like a light, like Elijah's wife
Herself, two flaming chairs, a double chariot of fire.
That's how I'd like to remember Mother.
Not, as I now must, waiting in all afternoon. I might have been
In Worthing. Mother, of course, would be gone
To the corner of Jerningham Road
To choose bricks from the yard
For the outhouse Father began in nineteen hundred and six.
Mother loved choosing bricks.
I suppose they would meet, herself, the upholsterer,
Waiting to cross between motor-cars.
She'd notice the bodkin stuck in his hat.
She used to tell Father about it at night
In their room. *Did you notice*
The bodkin? she'd ask, undoing her bodice
And all those buttons, his buttons,
Her buttons of bone.

The English Widow

(after 'La Dame dans le Train ou la Veuve' by Léon Spilliaert)

My life that day was – lank, borne.
I was led to a bench in the waiting-room.
I was led into the garden.
My life with him had been hard-won.
Parts of it, like small planks, fitted together.
Later I needed a woollen gown for all weathers.
It was mildewed with mud at the hem.
'Weeds' my mother said in my mind.

I walked out in the autumn wind.
I walked to the station somewhere in Belgium.
It had been my husband's homely land, then mine.
I abandoned the portrait Léon had made of the garden.
Apples lay on the ground, in the long grass, hidden.
A low wind hovered over them.
To what end were all things given?

The Silk Light of Advent

Mara sighs over the silks laid out on the rosewood windowsill.
She would rather look into the fire.
It is terribly hard to decide when the garden is dead.
In December the lake is dumb.
There are no leaves left and no wind left to stir them.
Later in life she will say that the light on the Somme was like that then.
Mara sighs over the skeins.
She is neither girl nor woman.
Her brother is in uniform.
There is no one left to walk with in the morning.
Her mother has always left her alone.
The newspaper's forbidden.
The angel will be embroidered, soon, by evensong.
After that there'll be no more sewing.
In the beginning needles were made of bone.
The angel will come in the afternoon.
Later in life she will know the value of precision.
At two o'clock in the afternoon she will say again and again.
Her brother will not be missing then.
He writes he is learning to smoke and polish buttons.
She will get up from the fire.
She'll walk slowly back to the windowsill.
She'll know then that the angel's hands are dumb.
The eyes are gone.
There are sockets of silk she will never embroider for him.
The lake is dry, like bone.
The angel is terribly beautiful.
She won't be able to cry.

the two of us then   as if *the two of them*
unfallen apple blossom
dabble of light   white muslin gown

plate of plain bread and butter
and the may   must've come early that year
to Grantchester

to that tea garden   now and then   no road
and nowhere now to hide
the pollarded

willow   the Cam
the abrupt stump of the Somme
the wounded in the university garden

the wind
the unending   black almost   bloodless land
I have found

Anchorage

In Julian's alone unlettered hand
love takes the hard ground

dust of oak-
gall and the quill, the history of the soul. It breaks

an April into tiny unprotected revelations
of its own. It makes bone

flower like blackthorn.

Awkward Things (1)

the albatross
my father's deafness
dust under the bed
the distance, now, between
the eye of the needle
and the thread
the wings in the cupboard

Awkward Things (2)

Ely, the ship of the fens in its fastness
the camel and the dromedary
Christmas
that bits of it are in Latin
that we'll be charged to go in
that we're 'crossing the desert in a pram'
that we persist in going on

The Road Home

It is the road to God
that matters now, the ragged road, the wood.

And if you will, drop pebbles here and there
like Hansel, Gretel, right where

they'll shine
in the wilful light of the moon.

You won't be going back to the hut
where father, mother plot

the *cul de sac* of the world
in a field

that's permanently full
of people

looking for a festival
of literature, a fairy tale,

a feathered
nest of brothers, sisters. Would

that first world, bared now to the word
God, wade

with you, through wood, into the weald and weather
of the stars?

Village in County Durham, 1998

And now an angel passes like a bus, its scarlet side
too soiled with old advertisement

to be of use. Where men are
knocking down the old shirt factory

with ball and chain in the short December dusk, it will
break down.

In summer when the factory floor was strewn with dust –
it must have been asbestos – and the door stove in

again, the kids, their pockets and an old pram
loaded to the brim with apples, came

to lob for dear life
till the windows lay like lustres in the sun.

Now, where the wings, in late December undistinguished as the sides of
buses, stall

there is a scattering of roof and ritual.

Looking at Chagall's 'Solitude' on a Windy Night

And now as the angel flies away over the small Russian town –
that'll be Vitebsk –
there is no protection.
Neither the cow nor the man has the heart
to work up a tune on the old violin –
oh, one of those wedding tunes you'd hear at the back of the little town –
nor will the man again hold the moon in his hand like an always
almost lost solution or a dream.
Ladybird, ladybird, fly away home.
The man and the cow are sitting down.
The man holds the Torah in its tight scroll
like a parasol.

And now as the wind howls over this one-in-a-hundred-small-towns town –
something lamentable, something less, though it is tonal, than
a half-remembered tune –
now I lay me down to sleep.
May I be sheltered, hid, as if from the steppe
at the back of my unwed heart.
If there's a wedding, it flies away over the foothills of the Pennines.

The river, Yenisey

We do not make the journey any more.
Most of us work. That is a way of forgetting.
We do not speak of the nameless river.
It was an autumnal river, fast, rising.
It was full of the rain that had wetted our heads
                and shoulders.
It waited for the empty cradle we set upon the water.
Our cradles are full now. Our cupboards are full.
Our speech is meaningful, like money.
We are mute, literate.
We are in love with our own imagination, the name
                of the river, Yenisey.
We know nothing of namelessness, nothing.
Nothing, in due course, comes to us.
We came to the river, as I remember, the cradle
                scrubbed and serviceable.

Sorrow caught up with us, sorrow in its shawl.
We set it afloat.
Now we are lost among satisfactions.
Now we are literate.

Barclays Bank and Lake Baikal

The bank walks in at half past seven, dressed and unembarrassed
by its sponsorship of Beethoven, the best

of music, *Hammerklavier*, here in its own town
Darlington.

Demidenko, Nikolai, in concert, self-exiled,
walks out of another world

like one who's wandered, handkerchief in hand, into the town
to watch the hammer of the auctioneer come down

and then, instead, plays Beethoven
as if he were alone.

He looks like Silas Marner so intent upon his two thick leather bags of gold
he lost the world

we live in: cough, cold, cufflink and the ache and pain
of bone.

It looks as if the light, Siberian, is breaking slowly over Lake Baikal,
as if our ship of fools

and bankers, borne upon the waters
of a bare

adagio, may founder in a quite uncalled for and unsponsored
sea of solitude.

But not tonight, dour Demidenko, dealer in another world's
dear gold –

for Darlington's recalled. At ten to ten
the bank picks up its leather bag, walks out again.

Advent in the Cathedral

1 *Carol Service*

Lord, they are filling the aisles with gait and shuffle.
Lord, we have laid on carols

for all those with learning difficulties. We are an incorrigible
people,

Lord, we are linguistically charitable,
we are a Barbie doll. We have laid on carols for all

the disabled,
those whose faces are turned to the wall of the world –

poor likeness of, poor dear approximation to, the ideal.
Lord, our beauty is visible

or else, among the elevated gutters of the soul,
we're gargoyles all.

We'd lose our nerve at that, Lord, and not less than all
the gait and shuffle

of political correctness,
cleverness,

our old credentials.
Lord, we'd lose our credibility to these undecorated walls.

2 *Altarcloth*

Because this bone blue bare embroidered altarcloth –
stiff, almost, as an old truth,

as the self – holds
good, the sea stopped in its folds,

I stand, as if I'd stood for ever at the water's
edge, alone and waiting for

the one inheritance
of absence.

This morning, the moon at flood, its cold salt
light

incomparable.
Still

what I love's the equivocal thought of the sea,
the sepulchre

of that small chapel on a point
in Dorset.

I imagine St Aldhelm, steeped in prayer, in doubt
stepped out

over the salt-dry sill
of the soul

into the cold incomparable air.

Arvo Pärt in Concert, Durham Cathedral, November 1998

Sea-otters will be calving soon about the Farnes.

Perhaps you'll go there, in your coat, tonight.
Perhaps you'll go to Coldingham

or Lindisfarne, or, landlocked, wait, as if
you too were

sandstone: wounded, worn by wind, rain, light.

O Lord, enlighten my heart which evil desires have darkened

where the imperturbable pillars stand.

For you have fidgeted through sermons.

Hard to sit still with all your insufficiency about you, isn't it?

But you will listen through your permeable skin as if
this music were

slow wounding, swearing in, osmosis.

Ebba, abbess of Coldingham, will find her nuns forsaken, fidgeting,

but you, as Cuthbert, suffering for all, will make straight
for the sea, to stand all night
waist-deep in it,

in praise and prayer,

in fret, is it, or under the stars' bare
scattering of thorns –

O Lord, give me tears and remembrance of death, and contrition –

until dawn. When you will kneel down on the sand.
Sea-otters will come to warm you then.

But you must be as sandstone.

Make of this music an Inner Farne where you may stand alone.

For it *is* Farne, from Celtic *ferann,* meaning land,

where monks will dig a well for you of wild fresh water,
where you'll find not wheat but barley growing on bare ground,
where you will build a wall so high around
your oratory, you'll know the sky, it only
a while

as instrumental, wearing-in of wind and water. Listen

then, you'll find your own skin, salt, intact
as Cuthbert after centuries of wandering, still
permeable –

O Lord, forsake me not –

and one, as Arvo Pärt in his coat, will stand before
the orchestra, the choir, as if he too had only now
walked out of water

new, renewable, knowing the comfort of sea-otters.

Strangeness

I

May it rise again
like the moon

from the sea
at the mouth of the Liffey

blurred by cloud
saffron coloured

for those who walk swiftly in darkness there
by the water.

II

May it stagger like silence
broken – by the glance

of bat's wing,
one dog barking

in Monaghan,
the pother and throng of my own

thought bothering
to put the boot in.

III

May it dispel
me and all

my affordable castles of stone.
May it come as famine,

faerie queene or fine
acidic rain –

or come at all, as if it were the soul's full
creel.

Meditation

I said to my soul: be still and wait
where the light green sediment collects

at the lake's near edge.
An old red lifebelt hangs in silence, sedge-

still. Still the long rope,
loosely gathered, loops

on its cast-iron post
like hope, at rest.

Held To

And now a little wind but little wind and stone and green –
grave-green

the pod of flowered-
already reed

or sedge –
and now, at water's edge,

a leap and tipple – toad, alone, moves
now, reminds me of

the little tinie page,
the page

in *Matty Groves*, who ran to give the game away
on New Year's Day

and now, but for the barest grace of balladry, go I
too hurriedly

beyond
this borderland,

this little hoard of stone, pod, wind
in the hand

that would hold tipple-
still

to

Annaghmakerrig
(for Bernard and Mary Loughlin)

It is the lake, whatever you make of it, lighter
    than Baikal, less alone.

It is the swallow that sped through my room by mistake
    like the sparrow that speeds from dark to dark
        through the meadhall.

It is the dining-table, long on its way to Liverpool,
    a *Lusitania* of laughter.

It is wit and water and that bit crack
    that's Geordie for *craic*.

It is gin and tonic.

It is murder (mosquitoes, of) before meditation.

It is the mock-grandeur of meditation, of honey
    suckle, baroque and bone.

It's the flight of the heron, the slow
    shift of light in Monaghan.

It is the quiet of Queen Anne's lace, of going
    alone in the lanes.

It is the lane lost among drumlins.

It is *go straight,* invariably straight, but the lane turns
    and the lane is always long.

It is the sorrow of Molly, of all dog.

It is the word *turfen,* the old word *bog,* Aghabog.

It is the church, not more than chapel, on the hill
    you must go the long way round to get to,
        merrily, merrily.

It is the abrupt dog Axel.

It is the Bible given to Susan Power
    by her mother in September
        1869.

It is the Psalter: dawn and desolation.

It is the uncovered love of David, loveliness
    gone of the Elizabethan
        word.

It is the bits of *persiflage* and *threnody*
    let softly slip by Bernard.

It is nonchalance.

It's silence, salt and bitter and good as soda bread.

Sunday afternoon at Maghera

I stare at the caves we've come too late to enter.

Already the sea is at home in them –
the strenuous, makeshift sea.

I am lost as to his need of me.

We walk in loneliness, the light
at Maghera

like milk spilt carefully.

We talk of five lost daughters, of his son, his own still,
undecidedly.

The sky makes shift.

I am afraid of Sunday.

I am afraid of the innocence of the sea.

turf
(for Marian)

the mountain silent after Phelim's gone

and ash like velvet on the hearthstone

and the comet with its great wind-sock of light

and ash like velvet, white

and shamrock, violet, hidden in the hedgebank by the stream

the bleak brown bogland

and the fire now slowly, slowly silting down

and ash that leaves our hands clean

neither one of us essential, neither one of us alone

Doon Fort

We have rowed round the bend in the lough to the island.
We have climbed. We have barely disturbed the dry, slant stones
of the fort. Or the late afternoon. Or the lough's rim,
root and stone. Beyond them, mountains.
Now the sun goes in. It is hard for us to be alone

with one another. Words have fled over the world's rim.
Imagination's fled. Is suddenly a simple wooden lid
that's lifted off to. Cloud reflected in the lough.
The silences of wind, of water. Swans, two pairs of,
their respective lough realms.

Inishkeel

Think of the unexpected helpfulness of water –

how it might strand you

on the small shore, here, as if this island were
the earth, its own frail sphere
of prayer

and obsolescence. There'd be tides and tides of
glittering small shells, broken here, like truths,
one after the other.

You'd be brevity, yourself barefoot.

You'd turn to salt as if you'd understood
the murmur of

the sea as missal. Yes, you might remember

gold or frankincense or myrrh –

you'd settle for the exhaled light of stars.

Sister Fidelma's Story

Lough Corrib came back to us, of course.
Father Cornelius said it would.
One day the land was inlaid with it again
Exactly where it should have been.

It must have come back on its own like a lost imagination.
No one was looking. Father Cornelius spoke of the moon
With its Lake of Dreams,
Lacus Somniorum.

Its reeds returned too and we knelt among them
In thanksgiving.

Then a paddleboat came proudly over the restored waters
Like a husband from Galway Town
To, as we thought, our own tidy household
Here in Annaghdown.

It cut across the wind with all its hatches open.
Water ran over its lower deck like a tongue.
'We are late, so late!' came a shout from its little megaphone.
'Please put the kettle on!'

Things that are early

Lilith who lived before Eve
my birth, by five days
the cobweb across my path
illness in my mother's life, illness in my own
the wind on the downs
Maiden Castle
the star, before its own light, gone

Tabitha and Lintel: An Imaginary Tale

Until the day break, and the shadows flee away,
I will get me to the mountain of myrrh,
And to the hill of frankincense.

THE SONG OF SONGS, 4.6

Taby said on my putting a pen in her face Ya pitter pottering
there instead of pilling a potate

EMILY BRONTË's *Diary Paper*,
Monday 24th November 1834

LINTEL

Who is it, then, that imagines me out of my mountain lair
and into the habit of hovering, here, at the doorstone,
mornings, in the slant new sun, the cobwebs covering
a whole field like a shroud of butter muslin
woven, light and water, like a poem
coming quietly into being?
                          Is it Tabitha, my singing
Tabitha, for whom I am become a habit of the tongue
and telling? Tabitha named me. Tabitha brings me
bread she's broken from a corner of the nuns' new loaf.
She'll ask me for the story of my life.
Snails have crossed the doorstone in the dark night
secretly as nuns, at compline, in procession.
Tabitha brought me an old brown habit to wrap myself in.
She'll tell me there are too many steps between the kitchen
and her attic room. Tabitha has a narrow bed, a candle
and a mat to kneel on.
                      Later, when the sun goes down
I'll get me to the mountain, walking through the water-meadow
to the narrow wooden bridge, breaking off
bits of bread and eating them.
                          Whoever imagines me into
my story doesn't know who I am or why I won't come in –
though Tabitha bids me not be so alone.

TABITHA

Tabitha, arise I tell myself these late September mornings
when the light is shroud-thin and the moon – or maybe
there is no moon – and Mother Superior told me the story
of Tabitha, the other one. And Peter came, she said, *and all*
the widows stood by him weeping, and shewing the coats and
garments which Dorcas made, while she was with them.
Dorcas must have been my other name. A sister.
Tabitha, arise I tell the leavened bread.
It'll be fat as a clay pot or the thought of God –
and *Take it, eat it while it's hot* I'll say –
not like the little paper loaf they lift from the altar
and place on the tongue, as if it were a leaf, an autumn
leaf, a lone moon – thin the word *life*, as they say it,
insubstantial. I must have imagined that girl.
Whoever imagines me must want some sewing done.
Coats and garments – that was the other one. Make do and mend
in perpetuity, me, and the thread like broken string.
Wool cloth for the habits, calico the Lenten petticoats,
the linen underthings. Only the shrouds of lightest butter muslin.
Tabitha, rise and take the little loaf to her.
                                        Undo
the bolted door while all the sisters are at prayer.

LINTEL

Whoever imagines Lintel lifted her out of the *Flower Fairy Alphabet Book.*

Whoever imagines, met once, as it had been innocence, a midden
of worn shoes in a wooden hut, Maidanek,

and hasn't forgotten the smell of creosote.

Tabitha's sandals remind her of her old school corridor.

Tabitha met me, the first time, walking in the lane.
She was carrying letters for Mother Superior.

I didn't invent her, who, in the tale, will turn out to be
my adoptive godmother, childless Tabitha, she who imagined
her own immaculate conception and sewed a layette.
There was even a shroud for it.

I've a lair of my own without lions or nuns. Whoever imagines

me, may remember herself in a gaberdine coat and hat
lined up on the asphalt drive of the convent school
to see the Queen Mother – or was it Princess Margaret?
A day in September, clouded over, cool.

She's almost forgotten it.

TABITHA

My orphan, own girl, Lintel: the sea at the door.
I could not imagine her otherwise. The Holy Land
is hard and dry as the moon with its own dour
sea of serenity, *Mare Serenitatis*, Mother Superior's
tongue, the nuns at the end of their tether,
the end of their prayer Gethsemane, Golgotha.
Hers is the sea and the sea's is the last shroud
laid in the press.
                    Whoever imagines, wants
me reeled, like thread, a stop short of timelessness,
wants me to kneel on the mat by the narrow bed
in prayer and then, with *Tabitha, rise*, get up
from the unforgiving floor to gather the stars
in my arms, remember Lintel in her lair
and say *God bless her.*
                    Why dismiss her so?
The death of the other, my sister as if, my own dear
Dorcas with her *coats and garments*, opened
me to that which was and is
mysterious.
                    I'll not betray her with a mere *God bless.*

124

LINTEL

Whoever imagines me thinks of the arkhold, Ararat.

God, in naming it and Noah, let the unimaginable sink
the wife of Noah, naked, in a sea of anonymity, *Mare
Anonymitatis.*
          Whoever she was went untold, tameless
as the waters.

Mine is the arcane mountain of motherlessness, immeasurable
meditation.

Here the stars are undeterred.
                     I have myself disinterred the stars.

Tabitha, halfway up or down her convent stairs,
may not applaud me.
        Coats and garments she muttered yesterday morning.
She's said it so often, as if it were part of her prayer
or the telling over of beads they do there.

The stars are yarrow seeds or burrs that stick to the habit
of walking.
        I saw them
stuck to the shawl, to the indoor shoes of the newly widowed
woman I met walking in the lane.

TABITHA

Stars come in shoals these cold September nights.

She flits now, four fields off, a light wind
hollowing her habit, as if she were all sail
and hardly a boat to bear it.
          She will not be harboured
though I wait here, longing and looking out over the low hedgerows
for her, the bread in a cloth. It won't cool yet.

Loaves and fishes Mother Superior said.

The stars in shoals, the bread for Lintel in a disused shawl.

Now she sculls carefully over the cattle-grid at the convent
gate.
      Now she sculls home, as I'd have it, home.

The hem of her habit is wet.

And how shall I gather the sea in my arms?

LINTEL

Whoever imagines me went most reluctantly to school.

I feel it in the soles of my feet walking over the wide
lid of Hell, though the cattle-grid bars burn cold
this morning, cold as the lid of the stove
or love gone out a week, a century, ago.
                Tabitha will
have nothing to do with the harrowing of Hell.

She wants me to walk in there, like Daniel.

She wants me to wear sandals.

Tabitha's full of tales.
            She tells me I could bring in coal.
The scuttles are small and it's only the parlour, Mother Superior's –
O and the big hall just at Christmas – where the fires are lit at all.
The nuns wear wool in winter and there's many a tale of
wickedness to warm the edges of the soul.

Tell me a wicked tale I'll say. *My feet are cold.*

How beautiful are thy feet with shoes
she'll say *or could be. Look at them –*
black as the bars of the cattle-grid but comely.

TABITHA

Maidanek, a middenstead, a mountain, enclosed, of shoes.

I put on our shoes as Mother Superior said the mad monk Thomas Merton said.

Whoever imagined my soul unmolested by love shall be interred.

Lintel can have the small guest bed.

LINTEL

The air of the parlour's been breathed already by Mother Superior.
It is crumpled and warm, like a bed. It has lost the austere
queer shroud of itself, of the room before morning
prayer. The shadows have fled.
                            I've to mend the fire
once more in there where the air is like Limbo.
In Limbo they live on stale bread and sorrow she said.
And there, as yesterday, will be Our Lady of Perpetual Tears
and a pile of letters under the paperweight
and Mother Superior with her heart inside her
habit, like an old brown teapot, breathing the air.
And I will murmur *Stella Maris, Stella Maris*
as Tabitha told me, *Star of the Sea*.

It'll be as if I'd brought the breakers in with me.

*　*　*

Healer

(for Nansi Morgan)

Like the heart or the mountain painted again
and again by Cézanne,

she will not mind what I mean
to myself or anyone.

To her, as to wind, sand and stars
or Mont Sainte-Victoire,

I shall come to learn
to be alone,

articulate. She will allow me to listen.

She will allow me to live without consolation.

things that are early and late

'the gold of the earls'
this pelican's foot shell
my own heart, hobbled by an unexpected tale
at eleven o'clock, a light meal
the moment of the sparrow in the meadhall
music written later, we think, for the sackbut or the viol
'this hardened helmet healed with gold'

SOJOURNER

(2004)

For we are strangers before thee, and sojourners,
as were all our fathers: our days on the earth are
as a shadow, and there is none abiding.

I CHRONICLES 29.15

To a Last

There's a lilt to the way you lie.

How is it to be old and looked at woodenly?

Waylaid, is it?

You'd better stay here, by the fire, like my grandmother.

In her flat shoe and her built-up shoe she wouldn't go even as far

as the river. You could have kept her company.

We'd have brought cobnuts which, this year, are everywhere.

Earlier Incarnation, China
(for Nansi Morgan)

Your legs ache now and then
remembering water, the rice plantation
where you walked, up and down, up and down.
Was it with oxen?

                                 Was your face thin
already, a dawn moon? Did you already resemble
the Bodhisattvas of stone I saw in a London museum,
the Buddhas of Compassion?

Catherine in Paris, 1910

My spine is my own in this light, empty room.
My father, Northumbrian.
My collarbone, broken – a stone.
The sea fled with me from home.

how the bicycle shone

and how it shone, she told us, like a little constellation seldom seen
and how the constellation stopped above the sugar-cane
and how, among the sugar-cane, they found the dark-skinned man
and how the man had been stove-in
and how stove-in was still the word her father used about the *Barbary Allen*
and how they left the *Barbary Allen*, by the water, by her lone
and how she was herself, much later, by her lone in London
and how London might as well have been the moon
and how the moon was white, like bone

Bethan

The cairn broke my head.
I knew the sea dearer to me than bird, breath.
I was a borrowing, Mother said.
Like Hilda, born and bred.
The stones of the cairn were strewn about the earth by God.
Hilda mended me like a cracked bird-bath.

The Harmonium

It had handpainted scenes from the life of Habakkuk under the lid, she said.
It was hauled from Merthyr Tydfil, to be hid.
Ivor Gurney was going to write for it, a half-Welsh hymn, but he never did.
Something like Hymn One Hundred.
He'd made a start, Da said.
Many times she had it mended.
Heart, she said, full of hope and humdrum under the lid.

Hester

Holly hardened, like her.

Her with her knees gnarled.

Who'd shadows of iron, honey, gold
in a drawer.

Who'd pans to scour.

Death held on through January for her.

For the hens in the yard.

She held too, like laughter
hoarded.

The Widow's Mite: Effie, Dumfries, August 1916

Bring out the boots that will no longer need to be repaired.

Bring them to the bare hillside.

Lovely is the harebell.
Still, frail.

I will take up my anger like a torn floorboard,
a bed.

'Thy will be done.' I said.

Dust of the August afternoon is everywhere.

Dust motes.

I'll gather all the holes together here.

A Shepherd's Life:
Paintings of Jenny Armstrong by Victoria Crowe
(for Jane)

Snowbound Cottages

We came to the border.
We came at night to Kittleyknowe.
We crossed her fields of snow
unshepherded. We did not know they were hers.
She did not come to her door.
In our house now we have lit two fires.
We'll be up for hours.

Large Tree Group

What wills her walking under these large trees,
the wire fence with her
and the world by snow accounted for?

Hat, coat, boots, heart
all right

now and long ago the small plantation where she sat
to work it through.

range and semmit

mantelpiece, her best, beyond her
ornament, amendment, more
the old range comprehended by her
her vest, or semmit, aired over the oven door
wood dried over the fire
october, november
behind the two clocks, letters

Winter Interior

Sheep in smirr.

Without shadow now, the snow,
the straw strewn by her.

She reads indoors.

Words grow smaller.

The kettle on the stool waits with her
through winter.

Celebration for Margaret, the Fraser Boy and All the Rest

On the mantelshelf, a rocking-chair.
A soldier with red lips, a trumpeter.
A picture, her father perhaps, a shepherd before her.
Farm of Fairliehope, near Carlops.
Carnations and poppies in a jar.
Poppies like sunk ships.
A spaniel, its front paws on an opened letter.

Jenny at Home

What shall we do with the days wherein we have dwelt,
                                    my bonie Dearie?

Days of your father, anywhere out on the moor.

Days of salt and straw.

Days of the stalwart woman you were yourself among yowe and wether.

What shall we do with the days, halt now but?

Hither and yon.

                                    Ca' them home,
my bonie Dearie, that have been well borne.

Airspun Powder and Bailer Twine

Air explores earth, its everyday alterations.
But the horse, alone on its stand.
The long-handled jar is alone, after its long association with her.
The japanned box of airspun powder.
The white plastic flowers.
Snow disappears.
But the bailer twine, kept, in a loose, useful ravel.

In Miss Macauley's Class
(for John Hudson)

we wear the great war of the world about our shoulders
      with impunity. Our words
            are borrowed

from the campaign dead:
      O bloody, bloody, bloody.
            Who's pinched my bloody kettle? 's what we said.

We're part of the hoard of what happened
      at Gallipoli.
            Gallipoli.

Wherever the avid crowd of the dead has drifted
      with its light war-gear
            of laughter,

there we are.
      Wherever.
            Stars, like salt, thrown over the shoulder.

Poppa

He liked to lay down a tune as if it were the truth.
'Morning has broken, like the first morning.'
Nothing broke him, Brodie Anderson Clinging,
not his son's death.

Euphemia in 1949

(for my mother)

She rocks the child reluctantly,
the cradle-muslin rough and thick with war
and, at the window, blackout.
London without light, almost;
bleak, her thoughts.

                                     Now through the smirr

her heart breaks, hearing her father
Brodie with his kilt-bright chords,
his 'Clouden side'.

'The Old Town Hall and St Hilda's Church, Middlesbrough' by L.S. Lowry

I am, like the sky, alone.
St Hilda's poor spire pierces me.
As a pen, paper.
Church-wardens like to turn the word *infinity* upon the tongue.
Take their hats off to me.
The old town hall has settled, now, among its files.
Buff-coloured, faded, from the beginning full.
Mislaid.
A letter from the Board among Christmas cards.
Dear Sir, we write to advise you.
1959 already. Middlesbrough.
People forget me.
Like a street-lamp in summer.
Or they were born yesterday and do not know that during the war.

Literature in Childhood

What was literature?

It was, like a dustsheet, shelter.

It was instead of a father. *Wait till your father gets home.*

Instead of a mother, washing alone.

Even instead of a grandmother.

In it there was no war we'd have to keep on trying to get over.

No corridors in literature, no nuns.

All the time, outside literature, fear was going on.

There were sandwiches, Marmite usually, Spam.

The Fifties

There were windows the war had left alone.
Imagine.
A world that would open.

Still

On the radio we're talking integration.
In the amicable studio, Christian, Jew, Muslim.
We are the children of Abraham.
The garden is full of arrival, apple blossom, bluebell.
The sheep are restored to their hill.
Even the road, momentarily, still.
Here we are then. Here we dwell.
Home. Dry.
See where the heron comes, taking its time.
It is Sunday morning.
Its legs stick out, stiffly, tidily.
Like someone learning to swim.

Esh Winning, May 2002

Currach

One there was who stretched the hide of heifer over my bare willow-bone.
One who, later, put my patches on.
One who loved his own long leather running-stitches.

Black Madonna

Her body is hollowed out like a boat.

She'll have carried Columba from Glencolumbkille to Iona

over the rough and the clear water

with the one oar.

Later he will bear the boat on his rough-hewn back

as if lifting her with her poor cold feet

over the tracks and stiles of Iona.

Lindisfarne
(for Michael McCarthy)

Let's not talk about
leaving the heart
to be looked at
like a script.

Let's talk about
the beehive of the heart,
the cuddy duck of the heart,
the heart's cuthbert.

Lay Brother, 12th Century

Among the whelks, that's where we were.
What would we have done without salt water?

When prayer was of no avail
we had a barrowful

of bowls to take it back
in. We were quick

at washing the wounds
in the Abbot's hands.

We had a whale
too, waiting to sail

with the autumn tide. It lay offshore
like God the Father.

Dottle, Donkey-man

Neither nephew nor niece.
During the war, lowered the ride-price to a ha'penny.
Ignored the world beyond the wire, as if sea only.
On the mantelpiece, a small clay one, given him
Glued together.
Lived, as if among deaf men, alone.
Dumb, like one walking into Jerusalem.

At the Friary in Alnmouth

(for Marian Goodwin)

We are looking at Coquet Island in the long blue evening light.
How awkward we are at Compline.
We have no habits.
The smell of the sea is in our hair yet, after supper.
Our hearts are stranded here, transparent, lit
Like jellyfish in the afternoon.
How awkward it is to be at Compline in the long blue evening light
With my old shoulder-bag lying there yet, at my feet.

The Fitting at the Friary

For hours, all afternoon, the sea is alone.

Who can help it?

He kneels at the hem of his brother's habit,
his heart.

Earth navigates. It makes its way among stars and nothing.

Could it ever not come home?

Earth's held.

The sea at the sewing-room door unfolds.

Puppet

There are many like me.

I was made in a world of wood and old wives' tales.

I was made, with rings in my head and heels, to hold only
the strings that held me.

Vaclav made me with his several knives.

His middle daughter made me with her milk and silver needle.

I lost my sword at sea when the captain ran off with me
in the play

and Sundays by the Vltava.

I was laid aside, like Czechoslovakia.

My strings were made of raw silk, red, and rotted
at sea and knotted themselves around me.

Old Bredow
(after the drawing by Paula Modersohn-Becker)

Speech is a garland: it doesn't grow.
He made me understand. The tilth
the heart's at home in is a burial ground
for strangers, still, a potter's field.
He kept his coat, its shapeliness and filth, about him,
all he had earned. He kept
his heart of spelt.

From the Artist's Notebook:
After some paintings of girls and women
by Paula Modersohn-Becker

Clara

She must have made up her mind about everything
before she was seven.
Her linen sleeves were clean.
She would have crossed the fields at dawn,
her father's fields, half-sown,
hearing her mother's admonition –
'Take nothing from the woman. Come straight home.'

Agatha

Life couldn't care less about her, I thought,
with her tidied hair.
Later, she'd lapse.
In her plain blue pinafore and unaware
of what I thought,
she'd traipse home through the water-meadows
with their small blue half-hidden flowers.

Eva

I don't know what she knew about it then.
She was alone in her heart, I thought,
more than half-alone.
She asked if I thought she was pretty.
I thought she was like a pale yellow flower.
I wanted a piano for her
and a father.

La Polonaise

Pale.
Parisian, probably.
Poltroon, they said, but then
they wouldn't walk out of their way to look at anyone.
Memory, gone out of her, of mother, God, man.
World without end, wouldn't spin
her.
       She could pose, with a poppy, earn.

Margarethe

What she meant was scoured stone
the churn stood on.
'Be earlier than bone or birdsong
if you'd idle like the sun
at noon,' she said.
She gave the lad not coin but caudle for his load
of advent wood.

Bette

And though she may have been the least Elisabeth
on earth, she bore a son, her John,
who would have loosed the latchet
of her shoe for love
alone.

      The way goes hard with her, of hearing hard,
who hoards his wild, too well remembered words
like marriage lines.

Ursula

'*Gemälde, Gemälde.*' She admires, ignores, the portrait.
Looks me over now, as if I were her daughter,
in the long dim mirror. Is a worrier,
a wind among the ragwort.

                        Is not yet
even loneliness in me, the child, and look, she's brought
a bowl of something hot, tart, from the near wild
other world. 'To warm the little one. *Gut, gut.*'

Tilsit, 1918

I remember the mouth of the river, my grandmother,
webbed and unwebbed winters that went with me
by the Baltic.
                  Once there was armistice,
an amber morning. She and I swept quietly.
There were soldiers. What could we brew for them?
Barley and water, bitter small beer.

German Woman, 1945

The war ran into me, like all women.
It made me a light tin spoon.
I was stranded among them,
Soldaten, Soldaten.
I wore a shawl of cloud-coloured wool.
I lived hard by.
How little their marching mattered to me.
Their laughter bruised my bones.

Poland in My Grandmother's Mind

In my grandmother's mind the winter in Poland's interminable.
Water lies in the road by the last potato field, the sky
so low you must stoop to avoid it like a lintel,

stoop, as you ride with the half-thawed load, your father's
war-dishevelled brother with you always
now, between shafts, to the house

that will lift itself, like history, out of the lost and level plain,
though the shtetl's gone.

Anna K., London, 2001

148

birds in snow

but that birds may be brought, without the brackishness
of the sea, to the too still snow
troubles me

The Belsen Man
(for my father)

He must have looked
  with his long loose shadow
like Christ on the cross
like the rag and bone man with his horse.

The Little Cello

Gdynia, 1949

The boat had faded and had no name.
It came with the evening tide.
It was awkward.
The sea brought it in.
It had one oar and half an oar.
The long and the short of it is, the man said aloud.
He was lame.
He had loose dusty trousers, like flour.
Her mother complained about the war,
about the flour.
The boat came over the turquoise water.
It came to Gdynia.
The sun slanted over the side.
The man rowed.
The man rested aloud.
She was about to be seven, she said, in September.
There was no bread to be had, no bread,
no parcel of bread from Poznan.
She'd something in her pocket, she said.
Something she'd.
Something she shouldn't have.
Look, she said. *It could be a soul, a soul made*
of wood.
It lay in her hand without a sound.
She'd found it under her father's pillow, she said,
in his kept bed.
Without strings or pegs, her mother said,
it wasn't any good.
He could exchange it for bread, perhaps,
in Lódz or – where was it he'd said?

Sojourner

What, at the end, was hard and worn and rounded
                                like the side of God,
like wood well turned, was home,
                                and must have been,
though, to my own mind, nothing but the old meandering
                                world and I lame.

I'd found all manner of thing in my father's barn –
                                harrow, rest-harrow –
though he was gone, like hired men after harvest festival,
                                the barn doors fallen,
the swifts not come.

Still there, the bowls and water-butts of rain, of sorrow,
                                gathered in.
Stored there, the spare sails for the windmill.

What was hard to understand –
                                the holes
in everything, the held wings
                                broken.

Child

She is heavier than air, a little heavier.

I shall carry her on my shoulder.

How did I come by her? Did I beget her?

Can I, how can I, abandon her to her stony desolation?

I shall walk with her as if I wore the whole Sahara on my shoulder –
wind, sand, sun and all of it frail as an aeroplane-
shadow and whole.

She has come to me.

'She is frail now, frail,' my mother said of her mother,
my grandmother in the cottage hospital.

'The light shows through her, she is full
of holes

and, when I lift her, lighter, almost,
than air.'

The New Broom
(for my mother)

Sarah, Alice she may have been –
servant to Julian of such long standing –

making her way among martyrs, cloth-merchants, men,
with her new broom.

Nothing will come to her now, a lost coin, a king.

Laughter – great leaps of it follow her home.

Avice to Thomas in Mid-life
(for Clara)

What shall we do with the morning light that lies like new cloth?
Shall we measure it?
Shall we make wedding-gowns?

There are, I'd say, a dozen Aprils in it,
though it is May now and we need not plight our troth
again.

Earth is but earth,
its rough and ready stone,
and the light that lies upon our shoulders lightly worn.

The Camellia House
(for Harriet Tarlo)

Mama made lace.

I did not think he would leave us.
I thought he could camp in the old camellia house.
Mama said so, loudly, at breakfast.

We liked the camellia house because of its glass,
its damp, flagged stone,
its cobwebs of wrought iron.

Camellias, she said, uncomprehending, old as bone.

A winter house, she said, in which a hundred years have gone.

Mama made lace.

I did not think he would leave us.

But he called for a kist of his own and a horse
and was gone.

Dolores' Afternoon

Mother's a bed on wheels.

We live among pomanders, within our own
  espaliered walls.

We live in peril.

We don't love anyone at all.

Like larkspur, we are largely idle.

Or like silver somehow we've inherited.

Sometimes, in our stead, you'll see a spinning-wheel,
  a wedding, a child born dead.

Dora, or Dido, buried beneath the yew where, later, we'll dawdle,
  examining arils.

The Lady Balaton and I

Her face is bare, as if it were of wood.
Her lace is made.
Long ago now she married the lord, my uncle,
Who rowed her over the ornamental water.
Where is her loud Hungarian sister?
Now there are only herself, myself, and a man
To bring in logs.
One day her heart will break like a blackbird's egg.

Wiltshire, 1931

154

The Flower Rota: May Margaret in 1953

Her thoughts, she said, were an abandoned crow's nest –
Gethsemane with Christ gone and the gate left open banging in the wind
and all the king's horses and all the king's men.

She came to the altar with cut chrysanthemums,
fern from her garden, twine,
tidy as a Guild in her apron.

The ship with her son had gone down outside Rotterdam –
dredger or merchantman, it was all the same.
She'd hang on, she said, like the last of the apples, wasp-bitten.

Exile, Newcastle, 1962

My mother, thwarted.
A Grand Man by Catherine Cookson.
Gran getting old in London,
the lino in holes –
'You'll catch your heel!'
The Flight of the Heron by D.K. Broster (a woman).
My first period.

Convent Girl

They wearied me with prayer.

In the darkening garden of the dene, I stared.

I sought him where the way was unprepared, a wild rose.

The old road with its white line will not come again,

nor my heart with its old-fashioned indicators,

but my riven father

who knows.

WOLF LIGHT

(2007)

I.

Wolf Light

What laughter, what lying-in among needles, is.

Before wilderness.

Before sea with its smelt.

Before sea, that simulation.

Before sea that, with moon, will abandon, abound in.

Wind in the forest, unamended, mere-

Dry. Spoor.

Heard

Hod: 'a basket for carrying earth'.
Who'd hoy it out?
Hester would.
Hester's a stitch in her side.
Hester won't bide.

An old woman lived in a shoe –
a broken shoe,
a shack of brown leather –
who waited for time, tide, weather –
a Tuesday Market Place shoe.

At Rest Two Roofs

The Wedding Breakfast

baked potatoes

butter, salt

a quart of milk

quick barley loaves

a dozen barrel apples

cake, Madeira

sack

The Hens

bara brith

Nan, barely –

I, by a hair's-breadth

heard –

barley about her

who bade the hens

here, here

among bedded stones

air

Mist

scant

    mantling

        miasma

      something the matter

morning

    man alone, maimed

        on the road before them

Something Old

who alone left me to laughter –
rules broken, after her, like bones
roles borne –
Nan Merthyr
who, among fields of yellow asphodel
gave rise to –

Bara, Brith, at rest here

Gran, my bower

Gone, the byre.
Gone, the milking-herd of her father.
Gone, the pretty maid of her.
Gone, the yoked buckets, her mother.
Gone, the carters, to the abrupt war.
Gone, Hartest, with its harvest supper.

Her Dying

world stranded, whole

    afternoons laid waste –

to whom Hartest, her wainful –

    all is safely gathered in –

whose earlier heart, my own

    set out

a Saxon king in his burial ship

    intrepid, without earls

Elsbeth

(after the painting by Paula Modersohn-Becker)

But for the goose that goes with her,
alone among days.

Days that wait, like dresses, for her,
like awareness, bare.

A rough field, fallow.
Birches, with their young leaves yellow.
Foxgloves in flower.

I in the big wooden chair.

There is no upholstery here but days.

Days that wait, like carts for the beet in November.

God has taken her mother.

There must be a house, an outhouse, somewhere.

It is 'their' goose, they say, that goes with her.

Unwed

Poor am I
as apron or as earth,
as bone bare
or as breath.

I then, bright-set,
an acorn in its cup,
had gone in by the yett
queen, deep, in velvet.

Narrow is now, a new moon,
new again.
Along the lane of life I've known
nor man nor wean.

Worn am I
as laughter or as leaf
in winter,
thin.

Sojourn

The fettered hill.
The skull.
Old stone, among nettles fallen, near.
Her light brown hair.
The brief bales.
The bared hills, the load-bearing hills, the hills of Lammermuir.
Her coming headlong here.

Shepherd's Law, Northumberland

the road to alston

from here, seven miles and a quarter

by river, by grid, by the opened
side of the fell

by ash, by alder

by the road, upheld, to the house with the peel-tower
where the world

light rides upward

ridden, the dale

iron inheres
as innocence, absence, old
as the heart, beholden

where neither car nor horse-drawn vehicle

side before snow

where late the sweet birds

where the one thorn leans in to the other

Tow Law bare

what lattices of light we are

the wood, dour, girded
with buds

Verger, Winter Afternoon, Galilee Chapel

Careful, here,

as polishing cloth across a floor,
police officer,
voyeur.

Air closes over the angel's departure.
Always, in the air. The river
in the floor

inhabits it, as light inhabits water
or the heart's interior
or here.

Durham Cathedral, March 2004

Woman Meditating

As an egg, hidden.

As a heap of straw still waiting to be spun.

The heart at its wheel, alone.

Laughter knocks on the wall.

Soon, soon.

Soon will be sudden and big as Gabriel.

Magdalene

Muddled, of lore, of bone.

Meddlers, guddlers.

Laughter, come and gone.

Then said Jesus, Let her alone –

as the moon

attendant

with her pound of ointment

very costly –

Common, prostitute.

At Sychar

Now Jacob's well was there
and what was surprising was that He spoke to her,
that He tested the truthfulness in her,
a woman of Samaria,
frail as the world or the waterpot she would leave there,
that He tasted the truth in her, like water.

Tabitha

In my sark lain.

Let me now go to the field, and glean —

Peter came.

Earth broke out in me again,
its breath, bone.

Heard talk of her, Mary, his mother —

among widows here —

knew, when I woke, I'd be healed black and blue, like her.

Black Madonna

stoup

a washen step

        stone

ingatestone

a shoal, a shawl

of stars you'd pull around your shoulders

cold earth-caul

clou de girofle

where love, accumulate and quiet

clove-quiet

Sophia

she wears a fool's cap, bells

silver bells, cockle-shells

a rose already in her dark lapel

she's royal, like rain

royal in her reiteration

Mary, Mary, quite contrary

royal in her uprooting of my own

II.

In memoriam Kit Allnutt

(1924-2004)

Christmas 2004

Thornham Parva
        and the heart, stone, unadorned.

Attenuation

In the shed, unopened, her parents' piano.
She must have set her heart
Aside then, like a nocturne,
Like a turquoise
Stone.
She must have said she'd wait.

Like a circle dance she would wait.
Like a piano,
Patient. Like a stone,
Silent. Like a heart,
Hidden. Like the Baltic, turquoise
And quiet, like a nocturne.

No more would she tender that nocturne
To the night. Let it wait.
Let the sky, inattentive, turquoise,
Stall. Let her, alone at the piano,
Fail, like a heart,
Like a fossil, caught, in stone.

Like a birdbath of stone,
Like a brother, numb, an unnumbered nocturne,
Like a bird in a strawberry net, a heart,
Like a lady's maid: she would wait
By her parents' piano
Wearing the turquoise

Gown she wore to go away in, turquoise
Like an old Armenian or Turkish stone.
She would work at waiting, like a poor piano
Player at a nocturne.
She would have a long uncomfortable wait
Like that of the heart.

She would be unbelonging borne, a heart.
She would be strung, like turquoise.
She would wait
By water, on a bare hill, like a bald stone
Circle. She would be beheld. Or, like a nocturne
She'd be known, an old piano.

Long in the waiting would she be, my mother, sullen, so, a stone,
A heart, lapsed, a turquoise
Gown, a nocturne, even, through the uneven night, a piano.

174

Marriage

as if it had come to the house from Harrods

as if with its lid and its bald études

it could hold and harm her

like rheumatic fever

like a summer

like the loose skin on a hand

it wasn't something anyone could mend

My Mother's Bedroom

Her cheval-mirror, her chevalier, her chest of drawers.

Dust-gatherers, like us. For whom I fear.

My father, hard of hearing, honed.

Something must have happened.

Where stars, gathered together.

Their silence, a silk road.

They are subdued, in whom darkness wells.

My mother washes her hands, as usual, in hospital.

Her books, small dry citadels.

Above Barningham

Alone, the moor-long afternoon.

A long time now, my mother's eaten nothing.

Ulcers of the mouth and meditation
burn.

What can come of heather, of the haul of being here,
of the air?

Bee, at an angle, a small aeroplane.
At an angle to her.

Mother

Herself, my heart's Sahara.

Menhir.

Madam, Sophie called her,

Madam. Stabat. Mater.

Nothing beside remains.

Last night I dreamt I went to Tessalit or Tamanrasset,
travelling alone.

the great rift valley

across which you walk, alway, from us

skin and bone, borne lightly now, as if you were

across which you, the sun, the moon, like famine, merciless

across which, straitly, you, forsaken, walk alway, as if

among mimosa, here or there

the crooked river-bed, the road toward

the perpendicular

Wold Over

Where would we go in our wooden shoe?
With her.

But she to her ready Lord was bound alway
and we

who —
proud, provisional,

our hand abundant yet in bitter almond, say,
or buttonhole —

She rode away over the dry flood of the world,
her one bald eye —

as if, wold over,
we —

whose Lord of indigo and gold

house, after her death

like Pegasus

among grasshoppers, stars, an acceptable house

Huguenot, light in its loveliness, hospitable

light that holds, like loss

atelier light

new wools, like worlds in waiting

women, with worn soles, walk among

cricket-quiet

not a workhouse, not a wooden horse

my old jacket

soon her small blue cotton stitches will be gone again

like stars in the morning

not, like the obliterated moon

not, like the dining-room

where she sat darning, shoulder-thin, old denim for me

on a summer afternoon

not, like her own utility

abruptly

with the sideboard, the cardboard, the cotton, the auctioneer's man

Easter 2004, Winchester

I walk with the bald day of her burial,
A holdall.
In the hotels it is April.
I walk with Neruda who'd like to lend me a bold long line, unsuitable.
I am abashed, that my mother – still.
I walk as if with her beyond the old cathedral
Wall –
As if with her, a parish church, a chandlery, on wheels.

Requiem for All Souls

Fragmented, moon, or mother, everywhere.

Succentor, woman, in whose solitary song.

A ship that came replenishing.

Whose body, gone to bone then cinder.

Moss as salvage, slow.

To lap a chaise-longue or a lady bishop's throne.

To lap a stone.

Where worlds row.

Men, like wooden gods, like war, go on.

Like stones and will not gather losses as they go.

Durham Cathedral, November 2004

afterwards

singing, a bowl of stone

the known, the unknown, constellations

round and round the garden

there are weddings, of wool, of bone

always is there

for hours

we listen to the worn asseverations of the wind

there is nothing to mend

III.

Good Friday

a day we stopped at, shyly, stumbled on
dainty with blackthorn

the wind laps at my ear, the moor,
the burnt, the bone-white heather

that's how I remember her

North: Sketches for a Portrait

Ragpath Wood

Alone.

At the top of the world, there's a wall of dry stone, broken silver, early morning sun.

Fumitory, grown
along, among.

Wilfreda, then,
who swooped on the world like a small hungry plane.

Who'll learn.

Newcastle Airport

Flat field white with refusal.

Frost.

Fever.

Wakeful hours of the night still with her.

Empty, bright as ether.

Will not resist.

Will not believe in Belfast, Budapest.

Shepherd's Law

Looks at.

Lammermuir. Cheviot.

Her own achievement.

Books.

Her mother, whose pride in her faded their covers completely.

Whose days are accomplished now.

High Level Bridge

The river is silvered, blown.

Come into its own, now, water of Tyne.

And who will remember when fields were closed, farmyards notified, long paths overgrown?

The river remembers the Romans and the heron.

Expects recognition.

A big red sun between girders of iron.

Stone

Brother, who is dead now, painted it.

Pent, there.

She brought it for him from the seaward shore.

Brought him bread and butter.

Brought him water in a jamjar.

Heron, he thought.

Heron, stood in water.

Wouldn't mention it, but.

For her heresies he gave it to her.

As it was, hunched over.

Coffee Pot, Old, Ornamental

Hands, now, hers, awkward.

To do with myself and the hole in the duster, both.

To do with the earth.

The floor.

Dinted she said to him at supper.

Meant it too.

Ever, lent to me only.

Mantelshelf, slipped.

I, slipped, moon in a tree.

Awry.

Stars, apparently, before they get here, gone.

Shine, though, where the pewter's worn.

The King of Sunderland

The king rose early. The king, alone.
The king slips in among the waters of the winter garden.
The king comes out of a dream.
It is said that Lowry slept in the town museum.
It was stifling. Blether and bone.

The king rose early. What ails him?
He goes about the herbal garden quietly.
Looking, as if in drawers.
He'll go upstairs.
He'll fall in love with the stars you can hear from there.

truth

lonely planet

loss, colossal, as the heart
cooled, hoarded

wolf, blue wildebeest,
abated

bear

in-house
a poor unlettered creature

floor
or

fosse, the way

the lone and level sands stretch far away

Museum, 19 Princelet Street, Spitalfields

old dull shades of silk on wooden reels
plum, olive, sky-
grey sea they, Huguenot, came hurrying over
hidden in wine-barrels

songbirds, windowsills

later, old leather cases, grandparental
treadle-machine
spool, bobbin
reel

old dull shades of glass, stained, skylit
synagogue light of iron
bare, barley sugar pillars, panels
plain

Lewis Brick died 24th October 1944   *£6.6.0*
In Memory by his wife and children

altar-gates, closed, with sash cord
chandeliers, kitchen candles
eagles, double-headed
chained

The Wedding
(after the painting by Marc Chagall)

Musician

little laid out

he led them under the canopy

wend away, road

wind at my shoulder

wind at the shoulder of the world

so little of it

shtetl

in a settled way of

wed

Bridegroom

I, the abashed, the groom
in my long, hired, indigo gown, my hat with its round crown, am,

having washed my hands of the world, gone
under the canopy, in.

Longing, like Noah's, a raven
that will not return.

Bird

I, bird, abrupt

Hebraic, born

of the groom

the voice of the bridegroom

of Solomon, the unremitting

of the inept, the broken

glass

Cemetery, Lódz, 1999

stalwart

awry

stones of Jewry

stars in the sky

where Noah

obsolete

villas and mills of laughter

The Clown

Imagination, bone.

He carried the porcelain moon in his mind
as if it would mend –

as if Belsen hadn't been.

Home

Air.

Papirosa.

During the war, paper –

What will become of him.

Bone, without reverberation.

Like his mother to –

Larkspur.

Day after day he'll look at the broken loom with her.

Malinconia

(after Ysaÿe: Violin Sonata in A minor)

The Abandonment

Who will abandon us now to the bitter aloes of love?

We have littered the water with boats like hearts unbidden,

like the moon, poor barque, with her borrowing.

Stars, like elders and betters, have left us to it.

Remote. *Geschwister.*

Remote in their leather gloves.

Chauffeurs, conferring in low, bred voices.

Voices off.

which, like blue cloth, will have been

among Saharas

where the horde of stars, powers, principalities –

where Bedouin –

where, known or unknown, *la douleur* –

among adventurers, Antoine de Saint-Exupéry, his aeroplane

Provenance

Bent little, bone little, broken down do little

Rotherhithe, Hither Green

Gran

Out of the ruin of Warsaw, white stone, beckoning

Baroque, white stone of the moon

White stone of Warsaw, Krakow, Lvov

shamanic

soup, milk soup

imagination

Altai, mountain of the moon

doubt

old dustbowl

'but'

mile-deep

Baikal

abyssal

Love

Among is where I am

and from whom

I watch you at the tiding of your own
imagination –

Begin, and cease, and then again begin –

at its slow disintegration
wondering.

One day I shall be shouldered
like the sun

alone, among, where I am
ever,

worlds unwilling –

they are more in number than the sand

Agape

There are gaps in thought.
The sun comes out in their hearts.
There is time for it.
Busie old foole, unruly Sunne.
A tree grows in Brooklyn or the Gobi Desert
Or in thought-gaps.
But they are an anachronism.
They are the inhabitants of a large asylum.
They live in their field of dream.
A fair feeld ful of folk.
They gallop, gallop and gawp.
At the end of their tether they stop
Like a municipal cup.

John
(after 'The Acrobat' by Marc Chagall)

You knew about old double doors
and stars, those dossers.

Your lot, to be lived in, a coat, a street.

Your tongue, an acrobat.

Your wit, a Yiddisher wedding.

Your heart, polite.

Painting Achille Empéraire in Winter

(after the painting by Paul Cézanne)

He stayed my hand who sought the silence in him.

The silence of his great forehead.

The silence of God once.

He made a chair for God whose legs grew longer every year.

It was upholstered.

It was hard.

It was an Upanishad.

We hoarded light like Mont Sainte-Victoire.

We announced our love for one another.

NOTES

BEGINNING THE AVOCADO (PAGES 19-40)

At Dinner (25): Sophia, called in her own country, South Africa, a Coloured woman, was a friend for the four years she lived in this country in the mid-1970s.

Beginning the avocado (40): According to legend, Queen Elizabeth I bathed only once a year.

BLACKTHORN (PAGES 41-70)

The Unmaking (45): The quotation is from 'The Wife's Complaint', a poem translated from the Anglo-Saxon by Michael Alexander in *The Earliest English Poems* (Penguin, 1966).

About Benwell (46), **After The Blaydon Races** (47), **Clara Street** (48): Benwell is part of Newcastle's West End and scene of some of the riots in September 1991. Lord Armstrong, founder of the firm that eventually became Vickers Armstrong, built many of the houses for his workers in the 1890s and the streets are reputedly named after his children, though in fact he had none. Dunston is on the opposite, south bank of the Tyne, as are Metroland, a permanent funfair in the Metro Shopping Centre, and Blaydon, celebrated in the song *The Blaydon Races*.

At the writing table (50): The quoted line is from Anna Akhmatova's poem 'Creation' in the sequence 'The Secrets of the Craft', translated by Richard McKane in *Selected Poems* (Bloodaxe Books, 1989).

The Swastika Spoon (53): When my father came home from the war, he brought with him a German spoon with a swastika stamped into the handle. Forty years later it is still in use in my parents' kitchen. His army regiment helped to liberate Belsen.

Bone Note (54): The quotation is translated from the Anglo-Saxon by Michael Alexander. See note to 'The Unmaking'. The poem is addressed to my violin teacher of 20 years ago, whose name I do not remember.

Saturnian (56): Mandelstam was born under the sign of Capricorn, as I was. Its ruling planet is Saturn.

Thomas Eckland (56): Thomas Eckland is an imaginary man.

Jehax (56), **Oboth** (58), **Cam** (64), **Morne** (65), **Egrit** (66), **Nailish** (67): These are souls who find themselves together in the Gathering-place-of-souls-between-incarnations. Each tells something of his or her most recent incarnation before forgetting it and going from the Gathering-place into another one.

Jehax has been an ancient African king. *Oboth* has been a member of an imaginary tribe dwelling in the forests of Siberia. *Cam* lived on a farmstead by a Norwegian fjord in the nineteenth century. *Morne* died when she was seven. *Egrit* witnessed an incident in the story of Etheldreda (*c.* 630–679), which took place during Etheldreda's flight, with two nun companions, from Coldingham (near Berwick) to Ely. *Nailish* lived in Durham some time after the lifetime of Julian of Norwich (born 1342), author of *Revelations of Divine Love*. In her book Julian writes, unusually, of God the Mother.

Preparing the Icon, At the Bellmaking (60): Very little is known about the Russian icon painter Andrej Rublev (*c.* 1370–*c.*1430). The bell-casting is based on my vivid memory of the bell-casting scenes in Andrej Tarkovsky's film *Andrej Rublev*.

My Cross (64): With thanks/apologies to Stevie Smith for her poem 'My Hat'.

Conventual (64): As a child Bede lived in the monastery at Monkwearmouth before moving, at the age of 14, to the newly-founded monastery at Jarrow.

Camaria (69): Camaria is an imaginary goddess. I wrote the poem during the Gulf War in 1991 when Saddam Hussein turned the oil taps on in the sea.

Ereshkigal in the Rocking-Chair (70): In ancient Sumerian myth Ereshkigal was Goddess of the Underworld.

NANTUCKET AND THE ANGEL (PAGES 71-96)

Fenlight (74): During the night of 12 February 1322 the central tower of Ely Cathedral collapsed. It was subsequently replaced with the octagon and lantern. The Latin, quoted from a record of the time, is translated in the text of the poem.

Delta (76): As a child, my nickname was Dick or Dickie.

The Garden in Esh Winning (76): My grandmother's son John was an RAF navigator, shot down over France in 1943. The night it happened, she woke and sat up in bed saying 'Something's happened to John'.

Fantasia (78): Morozowa was persecuted as an Old Believer in 17th-century Russia.

Rocking-chair (82): In his 60s T.S. Eliot gave up smoking and afterwards indulged in eating the sweets he had not been allowed to eat as a child.

Ocarina (84): Not disregarding Christopher Smart's *My Cat Jeoffrey*.

Untitled (87): Quotations are from Emily Dickinson's letter.

Table (87): The quoted line is from the Anglican Communion Service, traditional version.

Chocolate (89): The reactor core melted and fused into a lava shape that reminded investigating scientists of an elephant's foot. The Sarcophagus is the concrete shell erected around the exploded reactor.

Au matin (89): Beaurepaire is a ruin just outside Durham. It was the country retreat of the medieval priors.

Scrabble (89): The quoted line is from Rilke's first *Duino Elegy*. It translates as 'Every angel is terrible'.

Armagnac (95): Cézanne said he was 'sur le motif' when he went out, day after day at the end of his life, to paint Mont Sainte-Victoire.

LINTEL (PAGES 97-128)

A Letter from Marie-Claire to Her Sister (101): Though Marie-Claire and the events she refers to are entirely fictional, something of the life and work of Gwen John inhabits the poem.

Her Father in the Patients' Garden, Newcastle Borough Lunatic Asylum, 1919 (103): The hospital, taken over by the Ministry of War during the First World War, is now known as St Nicholas' Hospital.

Awkward Things (2) (107): 'Crossing the Desert in a Pram' is the title of a poem by Selima Hill.

Arvo Pärt in Concert, Durham Cathedral, November 1998 (112): The lines in italics are taken from the text of Arvo Pärt's *Litany*, a setting of the 24 prayers attributed to St John Chrysostom for each hour of the day and night. St John Chrysostom, a hermit, became Patriarch of Constantinople in 398.

While Cuthbert, born in 634, was a monk at Melrose Abbey, he visited the religious house at Coldingham, and it was there, according to legend, that he stood all night in the sea and in the morning was warmed by seals. From 664 he was Prior of Lindisfarne and, while Prior, spent three years living as a hermit on one of the nearby Farne Islands. In 685, against his will, he was made Bishop of Lindisfarne. He died and was buried there in 687. Because of Viking raids, the monks took Cuthbert's coffin and embarked in 873 on 'the wanderings', continuing until a final resting-place was found for the saint in 995, on the site of the present Durham Cathedral, which still contains his shrine.

Tabitha and Lintel: An Imaginary Tale (122): Tabitha is the housekeeper in a convent. Lintel is a girl of about nine who comes every morning to the convent door and is given bread. The story of Tabitha can be found in *Acts*, 9. 36-43. *A Flower Fairy Alphabet Book* by Cicely Mary Barker was first published in 1934. Maidanek, a Nazi camp in Eastern Poland, is now a museum. Thomas Merton (1915-68) was a Trappist monk and writer.

things that are early and late (128): Quoted lines are from *Beowulf*, translated by Michael Alexander.

SOJOURNER (PAGES 129-56)

A Shepherd's Life: *Paintings of Jenny Armstrong by Victoria Crowe* (134): The exhibition *A Shepherd's Life* was shown at the Hatton Gallery, Newcastle, in the spring of 2002. A series of paintings made over 20 years by Victoria Crowe depicts the life of her neighbour, Jenny Armstrong, who worked as a shepherd in the Pentland Hills and died in 1985 aged 82. The poems take their titles from the paintings from which they began. The phrase 'my bonie Dearie' in 'Jenny at Home' is from Robert Burns's song 'Ca' the yowes to the knowes'.

Euphemia in 1949 (138): 'Clouden side' is mentioned in Robert Burns's song 'Ca' the yowes to the knowes'.

At the Friary in Alnmouth (143): The window behind the altar in the chapel at the Franciscan friary in Alnmouth is of plain glass and looks out over the sea.

From the Artist's Notebook: *After some paintings of girls and women by Paula Modersohn-Becker* (145):
Paula Modersohn-Becker lived and worked in the north German artists' colony of Worpswede. She died, at the age of 31, after giving birth to her first child in November 1907. The poems were written as if the artist were reflecting on the lives and characters of her sitters. Each takes a particular portrait as its subject: CLARA: *Seated Girl*, 1899. AGATHA: *Seated Girl*, 1898/9. EVA: *Young Girl with Yellow Flowers in Vase*, 1902. LA POLONAISE: *Woman with a Poppy*, 1900. MARGARETHE: *Old Woman with Handkerchief*, 1906. BETTE: *Seated Peasant Woman*, 1899. URSULA: *Old Peasant*, 1903.
    Gemälde: painting; *gut:* good.

Tilsit, 1918 (148): *Tilsit:* renamed Sovetsk, in Lithuania.

German Woman, 1945 (148): *Soldaten:* soldiers.

The Belsen Man (149): My father's army regiment helped liberate Belsen.

The New Broom (152): Sarah and Alice were, at different times, servants to Julian of Norwich in her 14th-century anchorage.

Avice to Thomas in Mid-life (153): The Latin inscription on the Mildmay Monument in Chelmsford Cathedral, translated, reads:

> 'Here are seen the graven images of Thomas Mildmay and Avice his wife, but within their remains lie at peace. He was a renowned esquire, she a daughter and lovely branch of William Gunson Esq., and they had fifteen pledges of their prosperous love; seven whereof were females, eight were males.
>
> Afterwards, in the year of Our Lord 1557, and in the morning of the 16th day of September, Avice returned to the dust from whence she originally sprang, and on the 10th day of the calends of October, in the ninth year following, the unrelenting king of terrors triumphed over Thomas.'

WOLF LIGHT (PAGES 157-97)

Heard (160): *Hoy* means 'to throw'.
The Tuesday Market Place is in King's Lynn, Norfolk.

At Rest Two Roofs (161): *Bara Brith* is Welsh and means 'speckled bread'.

Her Dying (163): *all is safely gathered in* is a line from the Harvest Festival hymn 'Come, ye thankful people, come.'

Unwed (165): *Yett* means 'gate', *wean* means 'a young child'.

Sojourn (165): On the hill at Shepherd's Law is the Hermitage of Mary and Cuthbert with its chapel.

the road to alston (166): A peel-tower is a small square tower or fortified dwelling built in the 16th Century as a defence against raids in the border country of England and Scotland, with the ground floor used for cattle and the upper part (reached by an external ladder or movable stair) as living quarters.

side before snow (166): *where late the sweet birds* is from Shakespeare's Sonnet LXXIII.
Tow Law is a ridge-top village in Co. Durham.

Magdalene (168): *Then said Jesus, Let her alone:* St John, 12. 3-8.

At Sychar (168): See St John, 4. 5-42.

Tabitha (169): See Acts, 9. 36-43
Let me now go to the field, and glean: Ruth 2. 2.

Black Madonna (169): *clou de girofle* is French for 'clove'; literally, 'nail of gillyflower'.

Sophia (170): Lines in italics are from the nursery rhyme 'Mary, Mary, quite contrary'.

Attenuation (174): Stanza 4: My mother's brother was killed in the war in 1943. One of her aunts was a lady's maid. The birdbath in my grandparents' garden covered the entrance to the old air-raid shelter.

Mother (176): *Nothing beside remains* is from 'Ozymandias of Egypt' by P.B. Shelley.

house, after her death (178): Houses in Spitalfields, London, built in the late 17th Century and occupied by Huguenot refugees, have large attic windows to let in more light for silk-weaving.

Requiem for All Souls (179): On 2nd November, the Feast of All Souls, a mass is held particularly for the souls of those who have died in the previous year.
The Succentor is the one who sings the service – in this case, a woman.
In November 2004 a report came out from the Synod of the Church of England which suggested that women's progress towards bishophood would be slow.

afterwards (180): *round and round the garden* is from the nursery finger-game.

North: Sketches for a Portrait (184): *Ragpath Wood* is near Esh Winning, Co. Durham. *Shepherd's Law:* see note to 'Sojourn'. *High Level Bridge:* the Victorian road and rail bridge in Newcastle. Stanza 3 of this part refers to the foot and mouth epidemic of *c.* 2001.

The King of Sunderland (188): New Winter Gardens opened in Sunderland in 2000 near the site of the original Victorian winter gardens.

truth (188): Julian of Norwich referred to herself as 'a poor unlettered creature'. *the lone and level sands stretch far away* is from 'Ozymandias of Egypt' by P.B. Shelley.

Museum, 19 Princelet Street, Spitalfields (189): A museum of immigration situated in a late 17th-century house in an area of London that has hosted successive waves of refugees: among others, Huguenot, Jewish, Irish, Bangladeshi, Somali. In 1870 Polish Jews built a synagogue over the back garden.

The Wedding (190): *shtetl* is Yiddish and means 'little town'. A small Jewish town or village in Eastern Europe.

the voice of the bridegroom: Jeremiah, 33.11.

Sometimes at a Jewish wedding a wine glass is broken as the groom stamps on it to shouts of congratulation. In Orthodoxy it is a reminder of the destruction of the Temple; generally it is a reminder of life's fragility and sadness. Jeremiah, 33. 10-11 is read.

Cemetery, Łódz, 1999 (192): Łódz, known as 'the Polish Manchester', had a thriving textile industry from about 1820 to 1989. The 19th-century villas of the old cotton barons and the now derelict mills still stand.

The Jewish cemetery is the largest in Europe.

The stars in the sky is an old Sephardic song, *Las estrellas de los cielos.*

Home (193): *papirosa* is a Russian cigarette of rough tobacco with a cardboard tube.

Malinconia (194):

The Abandonment: Geschwister: (German) brothers and sisters.

which, like blue cloth, will have been: la douleur: (French) pain, sorrow, suffering – generally reckoned untranslatable!

shamanic: The Altai Mountains lie along the border between Siberia and Mongolia. Lake Baikal is in South-eastern Siberia.

Love (196): *and from whom:* The Book of Common Prayer, Communion Service. The Collect begins: 'Almighty God, unto whom all hearts be open, all desires known, and from whom no secrets are hid...'

Begin, and cease, and then again begin: from 'Dover Beach' by Matthew Arnold.

they are more in number than the sand: Psalm 139.18

Agape (196): *Agape:* (Greek) brotherly love.

Busie old foole, unruly Sunne: from 'The Sunne Rising' by John Donne (John Donne: Poetry and Prose, Oxford 1946).

A fair feeld ful of folk: from the Prologue to *The Vision of Piers Plowman* by William Langland, edited by A.V.C. Schmidt (Everyman 1991).

Painting Achille Empéraire in Winter (197): *Upanishad:* (Sanskrit) literally 'a sitting-down at the feet of an instructor'. A speculative mystical treatise dealing with the Deity, creation and existence. An Upanishad is attached to each of the four Vedas.

INDEX

Index of titles and first lines

Poem titles are shown in italics, collections and sequences in bold italics, first lines (some abbreviated) in roman type.